ON ZION
by
MARTIN BUBER

ON ZION

The History of an Idea

MARTIN BUBER

with a New Foreword by Nahum N. Glatzer

SCHOCKEN BOOKS · NEW YORK

First SCHOCKEN edition 1973
© 1973 by Horovitz Publishing Co. Ltd · London
Originally published as *Israel and Palestine—*
The History of an Idea in 1952

TRANSLATED FROM THE GERMAN

BY

STANLEY GODMAN

LIBRARY OF CONGRESS CATALOG CARD NUMBER 72-88533

PRINTED IN GREAT BRITAIN

CONTENTS

FOREWORD

BY NAHUM N. GLATZER

I

On Zion is based on a series of lectures given by Professor Martin Buber in Jerusalem in 1944. The original Hebrew edition appeared in 1944; the English edition was published in London and New York in 1952.

The author spent considerable effort on these lectures. In addition to rereading source materials he consulted an unpublished new translation of the *Kuzari* by Dr. Judah Kaufman; Professor Gershom Scholem translated passages from the *Zohar*; new Moses Hess materials, unpublished Herzl letters, and manuscript notes by Rav Kook were used for the pertinent chapters.

The date is important. In 1944 World War II was still raging; the threat to the Jewish people in the Hitlerite countries and peril to the Jewish community in Palestine was extreme. Hitler planned his 'final solution' of the Jewish problem, and the British administration of Palestine consistently refused entry to Jewish refugees. In February 1942 the wretched steamer *Struma* carrying such refugees sank with the loss of 763 lives. News of massacres in Eastern Europe and of death camps reached Palestine and the West. In May 1942 the Zionists, meeting at the Hotel Biltmore in New York, pressed for the recognition of a Jewish state in Palestine as one of the war aims. Terrorism grew in the Holy Land; the extremist Jewish rebels disregarded public opinion, claiming to use the only means available to the weak in a war against the strong. In September 1943 foundations were laid of the Arab League that soon was to declare that *de jure* Palestine was already an independent Arab country. There was no reason to expect the Palestinian Arabs to agree to any form of Zionism, or, specifically, to immigration of refugees.

These facts must be borne in mind to appreciate this little book, which, looking beyond the tragic conflicts of the day, beyond the struggle for bare survival, speaks of Zion as a sacred mission, a command to found a just society and to initiate the Kingdom of God. The book demonstrates the centrality of Zion to biblical life and thought—how it was dominant in talmudic thought, how it inspired medieval thinkers and Kabbalists, and finally how it moved modern Jews, from the lonely Moses Hess through the rationalist Ahad Ha'am to the saintly mystic Rav Kook (to whom Buber felt a special closeness) and A. D. Gordon, the Halutz. It has been said that Jews survived the terrors and tribulations of history because the ideal of a Messianic Zion was forever alive and refused to perish. Buber's work reveals how profound this ideal was.

This short preface can only point to some utterances in Buber's long public career that denote the seriousness of his attempts to give passionate expression to his idea of Zion, to serve it and Israel faithfully in a variety of circumstances. Be it noted, parenthetically, that the term Israel in Buber's speech does not refer to the Jewish state but to the totality of Jewish thought, teaching, and history, and to the people that experience them.

2

As early as 1901, Buber started to write on Zion, Zionism, Hebrew renaissance. Zion then meant to him internal liberation and purification. 'Not the improvement of the situation of the Jews is our aim but the redemption of the nation.'[1] 'Zion must be born in the soul before it can be created in visible reality.'[2] But only later, after years of study and reflection, does his attitude attain a mature form.

In an article, 'The Conquest of Palestine,'[3] he protested against the power of the sword in determining the fate of the country. The weapons of war may defeat the land, vanquish it; they cannot conquer it; conquest must come from within, as a deed of love (*Liebeswirkung*). Thus, 'when they told me the British have conquered Judea I did not believe it. I am determined not to believe it.' Only he will conquer it who, as did Israel long ago, will turn this land into the habitation of the Invisible One. True, Israel lost it, but the land waits for him who will reawaken it to new life. What is needed now is work that engages body and soul, the entire person; 'creative spirit, creative labor, creative sacrifice.'

[1] M. Buber, *Die jüdische Bewegung*, Berlin, 1920, I, p. 125.
[2] *Ibid.*, p. 29.
[3] 'Die Eroberung Palästinas', *Der Jude* II, 1917–1918, pp. 633 f.

In 1919 representatives of the allied powers meeting in Paris
discussed the European and Near Eastern territorial problems
and, in this connection, recognized the fact of a Jewish nation
and its right to an autonomous settlement in Palestine. Buber
shared the elation of Zionists all over the world but was com-
pelled to add a word of caution.[4] Will this Palestine be ours in
essence? 'Will we succeed in keeping the country free from prevailing methods of Western politics, the prevailing system of
Western economy, the prevailing styles of Western culture?'
(putting culture in quotation marks). Buber objected to politics
that uses power to expand power; to an economy that aims at
reckless profits; to a culture that is nothing but a well-ordered
public lie. In admitting prevailing politics, economy, and culture
into Palestine, the land will never be ours, he stated. True
Judaism, a Judaism grounded in original religious force, can be
effective only in radical opposition to these powers. The only
politics that is a must is achieving 'a lasting brotherly understanding with the Arabs in all areas of public life.' Our social
order must be determined by our ancient tradition of justice and
communality. Though the tradition about Zion speaks of a
sacred association of the people of Israel and its holy land, it is
the command of this hour to include the Arab in this communion.
Indeed, in Buber's view, the authenticity of Zion is being tested
by Israel's attitude to Ishmael.

3

Over and over again, Buber was impelled to criticize the trend
Jewish nationalism had taken and to point to what he considered
legitimate, true nationalism. As in an address at the twelfth
Zionist Congress at Carlsbad (September 5, 1921), the first Congress after the Balfour Declaration.[5] Whereas the chief debates
revolved around the financial and economic issues of the movement, Buber discussed the very basis of Jewish nationalism. He
criticized an ideology that 'regards the nation as an end in itself.'
Judaism is not merely being a nation. It is, in addition, a community of faith, advocate of the concept of the Kingdom of God.

[4] 'Vor der Entscheidung' (Before the Decision), M. Buber, *Der Jude und sein
Judentum*, Köln, 1963, pp. 508–514.
[5] 'Nationalism,' in M. Buber, *Kampf um Israel*, Berlin, 1933. English, in *Israel and
the World*, New York, 1948, pp. 214–226.

If the concept of people and community of faith are severed, we face 'national assimilation.' The unique history of Israel necessitates a 'supranational standpoint which must point to a supranational sphere.' All sovereignty becomes false when 'it fails to remain subject to the Sovereign of the World'—who is also my enemy's Sovereign. Of course 'the supranational task of the Jewish nation cannot be properly accomplished unless natural life is reconquered.'

At the same Congress at Carlsbad, Buber, representing the Hitachdut Hapoel Hatzair u-Zeire Zion, submitted a resolution concerning the Jewish-Arab question.[6] The resolution affirmed the will of the nucleus of the Jewish people to return to its ancient homeland, to build a life that was to be 'an organic element of a new humanity.' However, this national will was in no way directed against another nationality. 'It turns with horror against the methods of a domineering nationalism.' We wish to build a common home in a 'just covenant.' We trust that 'a deep and lasting solidarity' will manifest itself between ourselves and the working Arab people. 'Mutual respect and mutual goodwill' will bring about the renewed meeting of the two peoples.

After much debate a revised version of the resolution was adopted by the Congress. In a "Letter to Magnes" twenty-six years later Buber revealed his disappointment with the revisions —and the revisors—that watered down the strong version of the original. He felt that he had lost his effectiveness as a political leader and for many years withdrew from official Zionism.[7] Yet his endeavours on behalf of Zion continued. In the fall of 1925 he and a few similarly-minded men founded the Brit Shalom (Covenant of Peace) group. Its aim was the creation of a peaceful symbiosis of Jews and Arabs in Palestine as peoples having equal rights in a binational commonwealth.

To balance his idealist supranational position, Buber published 'Notes on Zionist Politics'[8] in which he called for sober, realistic statesmanship and for 'a healthy, determined pessimism, a nevertheless pessimism, a conviction that work and nothing

---

[6] 'Address at the 12th Zionist Congress at Carlsbad, September 2, 1921,' *Kampf um Israel*, pp. 327–341; *Der Jude und sein Judentum*, pp. 467–475.

[7] Robert Weltsch, Postscript to Hans Kohn, *Martin Buber*, second edition, Köln, 1961, pp. 435–438.

[8] *Der Jude*, October 1921; *Der Jude und sein Judentum*, pp. 476–487.

but work will bring about the decision' in any given situation.
Buber's realism, factualness and dedication to detail was rooted
in his being directed by the spirit and by a larger vision.

4

The real meaning of Zionism and the need for an understanding
with the Arabs were the subjects of Buber's address at the sixteenth Zionist Congress in Basel, August 1, 1929. The inclusion
of non-Zionists in an expanded Jewish Agency, established at
that Congress, motivated Buber to remind the Zionists of their
charge.[9] 'Israel is more than a nation,' he said, and 'Zion is more
than a nation.' Zion was once and still is 'the beginning of the
Kingdom of God over all mankind.' Zionism is a national fact,
but, more than that, it is 'a supranational mission.' As such,
Zionism presages a new type of nationalism which will have overcome the *sacro egoismo* of the current brand. Power politics will
be replaced by the power of the spirit that will initiate new kinds
of relationships between nations.

As an instance of the new, pioneering, nationalism Buber cites
the Arab question. The Jew, who has himself experienced rejection and alienation in his life among nations cannot adopt a
similar attitude toward the Arab. Despite the serious differences
between them a common polity is possible, since both love this
land and desire a future for it. Declarations and resolutions will
not help; action alone should demonstrate what we mean,
Buber demanded.

During the same month of August fanatical Arab crowds
attacked and massacred Jews in Jerusalem, Motza, Hebron, and
Safed; the riots took the lives of 133 Jews. The British court imposed twenty-seven death sentences. In the spirit of his humanist,
religious Zionism, Buber demanded Jewish intervention against
the carrying out of these sentences.

5

In an article in *Harijan* (November 1938), Mahatma Gandhi,
comparing the Jewish situation in Palestine with that of the
Hindus in South Africa, questioned the validity of the Jewish
claim to Palestine. The cry for a national home did 'not much

---

[9] *Kampf um Israel*, pp. 421–431; *Der Jude und sein Judentum*, pp. 520–526.

appeal' to him. 'Palestine belongs to the Arabs' and it is therefore 'inhuman to impose the Jews on the Arabs.' Buber answered in an open letter.[10] He faced the difficult task of having to explain the Jewish position to a revered leader of tremendous power who, however, had only scant knowledge, and even less understanding of the issues at stake. Buber tried to explain to Gandhi the main motifs of modern Zionism: Zion, he said, is a symbol and a prophetic image only because Zion actually exists; dispersion (Galut) is bearable only if there is somewhere a growing home centre. Zion implies 'a mission from above,' namely, the setting up a just way of life. This commandment of social justice, given to Israel at the beginning of its career, cannot be realized in the private life of individuals, but only by a national community. Indeed, the fulfilment of this task is the condition for being allowed to settle in this land. Exile, dispersion, came when Israel failed to perform the allotted task; 'but the command remained with us.' Now it is 'our one desire that at last we may be able to obey' the will of God, Buber declared.

As for Gandhi's statement that 'Palestine belongs to the Arabs', Buber reminds the Hindu that, centuries back, the Arabs, too, had come to settle in Palestine. What counts is what the conquering settler achieves in the land. 'God waits to see what he will make of it.' Both Arab and Jew have claims to the country. We cannot 'renounce the Jewish claim—something higher than the life of our people is bound up with this land, namely . . . its divine mission.' But it is our duty 'to honour the claim which is opposed to ours and to try to reconcile both claims.'

The Jew brings with him love of the land and faith in its future. 'Since such love and such faith are surely present on the other side as well, a union in the common service of the land must be within the range of possibility.'

There was no reply. Did Gandhi realize that Buber's letter (and a similar epistle by Judah Magnes) was not an exercise in nationalist theory but—ultimately—a serious cry for sympathy and help? Probably not. Was he taken aback by the religious, even sacral, mode of the message? Be this as it may, the Jewish spokesmen were left to cultivate their love and faith—alone.

[10] Brief on Gandhi, Zurich, 1939; English, Gandhi's letter and Buber's reply in M. Buber and J. Magnes, *Two Letters to Gandhi*, Jerusalem, 1939; abridged in M. Buber, *Israel and the World*, pp. 227–233.

6

Buber's testimony before the Ernest Bevin appointed Anglo-
American Committee of Inquiry in Jerusalem (March 14, 1946)
gave him still another opportunity to speak up on behalf of a bi-
national Palestine.[11] However, before stating this political goal
he spoke of the meaning of this land to the Jewish people. From
its very beginning this people was confronted with a task 'to
establish in Canaan a model and just community.' The biblical
prophets 'interpreted this task as obliging the community to send
streams of social and political justice throughout the world,' an
activity that was to lead 'towards the advent of the Kingdom of
God on earth, an activity in which all the peoples were to
cooperate.' This Messianic impulse was the force behind
attempts to reshape public life in medieval Christianity. With
this heritage modern Judaism could not possibly 'create another
national movement of the European type.' Zionism aims at 'the
creation of a genuine and just community on a voluntary basis.'
Such activity 'will show the world the possibility of basing social
justice upon voluntary action.' While stressing the Zionist
demand for the self-determination of the Jewish community,
Buber emphasized that 'independence of one's own must not be
gained at the expense of another's independence.' The command
of justice refers to 'the future of this country as a whole.' Jewish
immigration shall in no way violate 'the fundamental rights of
the Arab people.' The demand for autonomy 'does not . . .
necessarily lead to the demand for a "Jewish State".' Robert
Weltsch calls Buber's statement 'the last battle before retreat of
the non-political, spiritual Zionism.'[12] In November 1947, the
United Nations decided to partition Palestine, a solution which
Buber considered unfortunate. On May 14, 1948, Israel proclaimed its existence as a sovereign state. The realist in Buber
'accepted' the state; now the spirit had to be served from this
new basis.[13]

7

Buber made liberal use of the terms 'spirit,' 'spiritual life,'
'spiritual force,' to the chagrin of both his critics and some of

[11] M. Buber, J. L. Magnes, M. Smilansky, *Palestine a Bi-National State*, New York,
1946, pp. 32–36.
[12] Postscript to Hans Kohn, *Martin Buber*, p. 444.
[13] 'The Way of Israel,' *Congress Weekly*, September 8, 1958.

his followers who pressed for a clear-cut definition of the terms. Buber, on the other hand, expected his readers to respond to his sensitivity by their own intuition. Occasionally, however, he became somewhat more explicit, as (in 1919) when speaking of the new commonwealth to be built in the Land of Israel.[14] Turning against the 'exclusively political-minded' he demanded that the new commonwealth become not just another of the many small states. Only 'if it becomes a spiritual force will it endure.' Buber makes it clear that the term does not mean 'intellectual standards or cultural achievements.' What it does mean is 'an overcoming the dualisms of truth and reality, idea and fact, morals and politics.' Or, with greater clarity: Spiritual force means 'the substitution for war by community,' the practice of 'the religion of communal living.' Such lived religion is the only spiritual force that 'can withstand the impact of our times.' A Zion so based will become 'the new sanctuary of the nations' and the people that once pioneered in the realization of this idea 'will become the priest' in that sanctuary. And again: The true community will not arise out of 'the vacuum of intellectualism' but out of the 'exalted commandment, preserved in our memory and internal history.' This is our 'spiritual heritage.'

In the same address Buber defined spirit as 'the prophetic teacher of faithfulness and renewal,' and 'admonisher of men to be faithful to the task of realization' of the genuine community, 'a guardian of social dynamics out of which all institutions and communal forms must renew themselves.'

Buber spoke of the spiritual force and its implications in full awareness of the odds confronting him and those who cared to listen: the rigorism of the traditionalists, the indolence and doctrinarism, egotism and vanity, the cult of the 'pure idea' and the cult of *Realpolitik*. Undeterred by disappointments past and present, he was 'certain of Israel' and ready to respond to the call of the spirit and to the command issuing from Zion. The present volume, written in a time of anguish, documents the power of the idea of Zion in the internal history of Israel.

[14] 'Der heilige Weg' (The Holy Way), Frankfurt am Main, 1919; English, M. Buber, *On Judaism*, New York, 1967, pp. 108–148.

PREFACE

The Hebrew edition of this book appeared in 1944. In May 1948 the State of Israel was proclaimed, but it has not proved necessary to alter anything in the text of the present work, which is intended to shed light not on the history of a political enterprise but on that of a religious idea or rather on the spiritual history of a faith. How much of the latter the political enterprise and its consequences will be able to realize will naturally be revealed only in the course of several generations. But it is only right that, as long as such a spiritual reality lives, history should be responsible to it rather than that it should be responsible to history.

MARTIN BUBER

Jerusalem, Spring 1950

INTRODUCTION

ZION AND THE OTHER NATIONAL CONCEPTS

IT is impossible to appreciate the real meaning of 'Zion' so long as one regards it as simply one of many other national concepts. We speak of a 'national concept' when a people makes its unity, spiritual coherence, historical character, traditions, origins and evolution, destiny and vocation the objects of its conscious life and the motive power behind its actions. In this sense the Zion concept of the Jewish people can be called a national concept. But its essential quality lies precisely in that which differentiates it from all other national concepts.

It is significant that this national concept was named after a place and not, like the others, after a people, which indicates that it is not so much a question of a particular people as such but of its association with a particular land, its native land. Moreover, the idea was not named after one of the usual descriptions of this land—Canaan or Palestine or Erets-Israel—but after the old stronghold of the Jebusites which David made his residence and whose name was applied by poets and prophets to the whole city of Jerusalem, not so much as the seat of the royal fort, however, but as the place of the sanctuary, just as the holy mountain itself is often so called : quite early on the name was constructed as that of a holy place. Zion is 'the city of the great King' (Psalms 48, 3), that is of God as the King of Israel. The name has retained this sacred character ever since. In their prayers and songs the mourning and yearning of the people in exile were bound up with it, the holiness of the land was concentrated in it and in the Cabbala Zion was equated with an emanation of God Himself. When the Jewish people adopted this name for their national concept, all these associations were contained in it.

This was inevitable, for, in contrast to the national concepts of other peoples, the one described by this name was no new invention, not the product of the social and political changes manifested by the French Revolution, but merely a continuation, the re-statement of an age-old religious and popular reality adapted to the universal form of the national movements of the nineteenth century. This reality was the holy matrimony of a 'holy' people with a 'holy' land, the local point of which was the name of Zion.

It has been one of the disastrous errors of modern Biblical criticism to attribute this category of the Holy, as applied in the Scriptures to the people and the land, to the sacerdotalism of a later age for which the claims of public worship were all-important. On the contrary, it appertains rather to the *primitive* conception of the Holy as we find it in tribes living close to nature, who think of the two main supports of national life, man and the earth, as endowed with sacred powers. In the tribes which united to form 'Israel' this concept developed and became transformed in a special way: holiness is no longer a sign of power, a magic fluid that can dwell in places and regions as well as in people and groups of people, but a quality bestowed on this particular people and this particular land because God 'elects' both in order to lead His chosen people into His chosen land and to join them to each other. It is His election that sanctifies the chosen people as His immediate attendance and the land as His royal throne and which makes them dependent on each other. This is more a political, a theopolitical than a strictly religious concept of holiness: the outward form of worship is merely a concentrated expression of the sovereignty of God. Abraham builds altars where God has appeared to him, but he does so not as a priest but as a herald of the Lord by whom he has been sent, and when he calls on the name of his Lord above the altar he thereby proclaims his Lord's royal claim to possession of the surrounding land. This is not the transforming interpretation of a later age but has its roots in primitive language, analogies of which are to be found in other early peoples but nowhere in such historical concreteness as here. Here 'holiness' still means to belong to God not merely through religious symbols and in the times and places consecrated to public worship but as a people and a land, in the all-embracing range and reality of public life. It is only later that the category of the Holy becomes restricted to public worship, a process which increases the more the sphere of public life is withdrawn from the sovereign rule of God.

That it is God who joins this people to this land is not a subsequent historical interpretation of events; the wandering tribes themselves were inspired again and again by the promise made to their forefathers and the most enthusiastic among them saw God Himself leading His people into the promised land. It is impossible to imagine a historical Israel as existing at any time without belief in its God or previously to such belief : it is precisely the message of the common Leader that unites the tribes into a people. It is no less impossible to imagine this belief as existing before and outside Israel : it is an absolutely historical belief, the belief in a God leading first the fathers and then the whole people into the promised land at historically determined times for divinely historical purposes. Here is no ' nation ' as such and no ' religion ' as such but only a people interpreting its historical experiences as the actions of its God.

This belief in divine leadership is, however, at the same time the belief in a mission. However much of the legislation that has come down to us in the Bible may be attributed to later literary accretions, there is no doubt at all that the exodus from Egypt was bound up with the imposing of a law that was taken to be a divine charter and the positive nucleus of all the later developments was essentially the instruction to establish a ' holy ' national community in the promised land. For these tribes divine leadership certainly implied an ordinance concerning the future in the land and from this basis a tradition and a doctrine were evolved. The story of Abraham, which connects the gift of Canaan with the command to be a blessing, is a most concise résumé of the fact that the association of this people with this land signifies a mission. The people came to the land to fulfil the mission, even by each new revolt against it they recognized its continuing validity ; the prophets were appointed to interpret the past and future destiny of the people on the basis of its failure as yet to establish the righteous city of God for the establishment of which it had been led into the land. This land was at no time in the history of Israel simply the property of the people ; it was always at the same time a challenge to make of it what God intended to have made of it.

Thus from the very beginning the unique association between this people and this land was characterized by what was to be, by the intention that was to be realized. It was a consummation that could not be achieved by the people or the land on its own but only by the faithful co-operation of the two together and it was an association in which the land appeared not as a dead, passive

object but as a living and active partner. Just as, to achieve fullness of life, the people needed the land, so the land needed the
people, and the end which both were called upon to realize could
only be reached by a living partnership. Since the living land
shared the great work with the living people it was to be both the
work of history and the work of nature. Just as nature and
history were united in the creation of man, so these two spheres
which have become separated in the human mind were to unite
in the task in which the chosen land and the chosen people were
called upon to co-operate. The holy matrimony of land and
people was intended to bring about the matrimony of the two
separated spheres of Being.

This is the theme, relating to a small and despised part of the
human race and a small and desolate part of the earth, yet
world-wide in its significance, that lies hidden in the name of
Zion. It is not simply a special case among the national concepts
and national movements: the exceptional quality that is here
added to the universal makes it a unique category extending
far beyond the frontier of national problems and touching the
domain of the universally human, the cosmic and even of Being
itself. In other respects the people of Israel may be regarded as
one of the many peoples on earth and the land of Israel as one
land among other lands: but in their mutual relationship and
in their common task they are unique and incomparable. And,
in spite of all the names and historical events that have come
down to us, what has come to pass, what is coming and shall
come to pass between them, is and remains a mystery. From
generation to generation the Jewish people have never ceased to
meditate on this mystery.

When the national movement of this people inherited the
mystery, a powerful desire to dissolve it arose in spite of the
protests of the movement's most important spiritual leaders. It
seemed to belong to the purely 'religious' sphere and religion
had become discredited for two reasons: in the West, because
of its attempt to denationalize itself in the age of Emancipation,
in the East, because of its resistance to the Europeanization of
the Jewish people on which the national movement wanted to
base itself. The secularizing trend in Zionism was directed against
the mystery of Zion too. A people like other peoples, a land like
other lands, a national movement like other national movements

—this was and still is proclaimed as the postulate of common sense against every kind of 'mysticism'. And from this standpoint the age-long belief that the successful reunion of this people with this land is inseparably bound up with a command and a condition was attacked. No more is necessary—so the watchword runs—than that the Jewish people should be granted the free development of all its powers in its own country like any other people; that is in fact what is meant by 'Regeneration.'

The certainty of the generations of Israel testifies that this view is inadequate. The idea of Zion is rooted in deeper regions of the earth and rises into loftier regions of the air, and neither its deep roots nor its lofty heights, neither its memory of the past nor its ideal for the future, both of the selfsame texture, must be repudiated. If Israel renounces the mystery, it renounces the heart of reality itself. National forms without the eternal purpose from which they have arisen signify the end of Israel's specific fruitfulness. The free development of the latent power of the nation without a supreme value to give it purpose and direction does not mean regeneration but the mere sport of a common self-deception behind which spiritual death lurks in ambush. If Israel desires less than it is intended to fulfil then it will even fail to achieve the lesser goal.

With every new encounter of this people with this land the task is set afresh, but every time it is rooted in the historical situation and its problems. If it is not mastered, what has already been achieved will fall into ruin. Once it is really mastered this may be the beginning of a new kind of human society. To be sure, the problem proves to be more difficult every time it is tackled. It is more difficult to set up an order based on justice in the land if one is under the jurisdiction of a foreign power, as after the return from Babylon, than if one is comparatively free to determine one's own way of life, as after the first appropriation of the land; and it is still more difficult if one has to reckon with the coexistence of another people in the same country, of cognate origin and language but mainly foreign in tradition, structure and outlook, and if this vital fact has to be regarded as an essential part of the problem. On the other hand, there seems to be a high purpose behind the increasing difficulty of the task. Even in the life of the individual what has once been neglected can never be made up for in the same sphere and under the same conditions;

but one is sometimes allowed to make amends for lost opportunities in a quite different situation, in a quite different form, and it is significant that the new situation is more contradictory and the new form more difficult to realize than the old and that each fresh attempt demands an even greater exertion to fulfil the task; for such is the hard but not ungracious way of life itself. The same process seems to be true of the life of Israel.

PART ONE

THE TESTIMONY OF THE BIBLE

THE TESTIMONY OF THE BIBLE

THE PRAYER OF THE FIRST-FRUITS

IN the Hebrew Bible in which there are so many prayers, gathered together in the Psalms as well as scattered among the narrative and prophetic texts, we find only two that are prescribed to be said at a certain annually recurring period (Deuteronomy 26). The first of them is the prayer to be said at the offering of the first-fruits, the 'first of all the fruit of the earth' (26, 2). The commandment to offer choice fruits from the early produce of the land in the sanctuary recurs on several occasions in the five books of the Instruction. Here now, in the last of these passages it is stated how and with what accompanying words the action is to be carried out.

Gifts to the gods of the first-fruits of the harvest are a universally familiar custom, not least in the countries which influenced the ancient culture of Israel, namely Babylon, Egypt and Canaan. Prayers, too, from many different stages of development have come down to us, prayers expressing the purposes of the offering. The gods are thanked for the blessings of the earth; they are invited to the meal; they are asked to bestow new fertility. But of all the prayers of the first-fruits in the world that I know there is only one in which, in contrast to all the others, God is glorified for His gift of a *land* to the worshipper.

The opening instruction already points to this: 'And it shall be when thou art come in unto the land, which the Lord thy God giveth thee for a possession, and inheritest it, and dwellest therein . . .' Apart from this passage there is only one other in which the formula is to be found: the one in which the question of 'setting a king over thee' is mentioned (17, 14). But whereas in that instruction the people as a whole is addressed as 'thou', here it occurs only at the beginning in the preliminary sentence already quoted: the 'thou' of the following sentence—'that thou shalt take of the first of all the fruit of the earth, which thou shalt bring of the land that the Lord thy God giveth thee, and shalt put it in a basket, and shalt go unto the place which the Lord thy God shall choose to place his name there and shalt

come to the priest that shall be in those days and say unto
him . . .' —the 'thou' in this sentence obviously no longer refers
to the people as a whole but to the individual, each individual
landowner in Israel throughout all generations. The presupposition is a collective one, the duty a personal one. Furthermore, the presupposition is a never-to-be-repeated historical
event, the duty one which returns with every year.

This dual reference of the 'thou' is not, however, simply
incidental. The first words which the land-owner is to speak to
the priest show that clearly enough: 'I report this day to the
Lord thy God that I am come unto the country which the Lord
sware unto our fathers for to give us.' Even in the latest ages
the man who offers the first-fruits is not to say, for instance, 'My
fathers have come into the country' but 'I have come into the
country'. Here the people and the individual are merged into
one. 'I am come into the country' means first of all 'I, the people
of Israel, am come into the country'. The speaker identifies himself with Israel and speaks in its name. The saying 'I am come
into the country' corresponds to the reference to Israel in the
first sentence: 'When thou art come in unto the land: even
the son of a later generation speaks for the generation which once
came into Canaan and therefore for the whole people that came
to Canaan in that generation. But that does not exhaust the full
meaning of this 'I'. The man does not simply say: 'I am come
into the country'; he says that he is 'reporting to the Lord' that
he has come into the country. That can hardly mean anything
else but: 'I report as one who has come into the country.' Every
year when he brings the first-fruits of his land he reports anew
as one who has come into the country. If he were speaking
merely for the people he would not need to 'report'. He does so
because he is under an obligation to say: 'Not merely Israel, but
also this very person here has come into the land,—I as an
individual feel and profess myself as one who has come into the
land and every time that I offer its first-fruits I acknowledge
that anew and declare it anew.' To understand this rightly one
must recall another passage in the same book (5, 3 f.) in which
Moses says to the people, before he repeats the Ten Commandments which he once heard on the holy mountain: 'The Lord
our God made a covenant with us on Horeb. The Lord made not
this covenant with our fathers, but with us, even us, who are all

of us here live this day.' This sentence, which expresses the
eternal actuality of the covenant with such emphatic directness,
does not say: 'not with our fathers *alone*, with our fathers
who have meanwhile died in the wilderness', but more un-
compromisingly: 'not with our fathers': not with a single
generation, but with each generation of Israel that lives before
His face God has made His covenant. And just as the making of
the covenant is the concern of all generations of the people, so too
is the coming into the land promised in the covenant. This
acquisition of land is a gift of land, a gift which God is constantly
renewing. Every peasant in each generation of Israel, when he
brings the first-fruits, thanks God for the land into which He has
brought *him*. This 'bringing' into the land and that 'bringing'
the first-fruits are in fact set into a mutual relationship to one
another that is stressed in the prayer itself: 'And He hath
brought us into this place . . . and now, I have *brought* the first-
fruits of the land.' Thus is expressed the reciprocity between God
and the individual members of His people. The peasant says:
'I have been brought by Him into this fruitful land and now I
bring Him of its fruits'. That is something more than mere thanks-
giving. The whole land has been bestowed by God on the people;
the harvest which the man whom God has brought into the land
produces from the soil, comes from God's blessing and work, it
is impossible to give Him anything of it, but one can bring Him
something, the best of the first-fruits, as a symbol and for consecration. Even today a sacrificial formula of the Palestinian
Arabs begins with the words: 'From Thee and unto Thee'.

He, God, is the giver. As so often in the Bible, the heart of the
matter is brought out by the sevenfold repetition of the verb
'to give' in the passage containing the instruction and the prayer.
In the first three and last three cases it is used of God's gift to
Israel; between the two groups of three, however, there is a
strange 'giving', obviously not merely to make up the full seven
but chiefly to emphasize the negative background of the divine
giving; it is the Egyptians, who 'gave us hard bondage' (Deuteronomy 26, 6). Of such kind are the historical 'gifts' made to
Israel by the other peoples of the world. God's gift frees it from the
bondage laid upon it by the other peoples. But God's great gift
to Israel—it is this that the fivefold repetition impresses on us—
is the land. Finally, (26, 11) in order to prevent any misunder-

standing at all, it is summed up in more general terms: 'every
good thing', not only the land, but also its annual yield comes
from God as his gift.

In accordance with tradition the land is described as 'a
land flowing with milk and honey' (26, 9). No peasant describes
the land of his desire in that way. When the peasant praises his
land, he says: 'A land of wheat and barley and vines and fig
trees and pomegranates' (8, 8). It is not, however, this or a
similar description that has become the familiar one but the other.
Some think it is a later interpolation only to be found in later
texts and that 'milk and honey' refers to the sacred food that
recurs in the mythologies of various peoples; in this case the term
will have arisen not out of the basic feeling of an early and creative hour in the history of the people but from a romantic, almost
literary trend of thought. But it is not usual for sayings of such
simplicity and pregnancy to arise in this way. It would also be
more than strange if a later epoch were, by reason of some
romantic proclivity, subsequently to have given to the promised
land a name which expresses not the peasant's interests but those
of the pasture-seeking roving shepherd, in whom the old food-
gathering instinct survives and which expresses his delight in discovering the honey of the wild bees.[1] The saying refers to representative products that the land offers to the newcomer without
the need for any effort on his part: milk, into which the energy
of the rich pastures, as it were of one tremendous oasis, is con-
verted and honey for the refreshment of passers by. It is
essentially a very old saying, the expression of a promise made to
nomads or semi-nomads. In the centuries following the entry
into the promised land it seems in literature to have given way
to the peasants' new pride, although it continued to be current
in the oral language; later on, urban circles in Judea, especially
the clergy of Jerusalem and other nearby holy places gave the
saying a more prominent place in the literary language in an
attempt really to do justice to early conditions from a historical
point of view and in so doing they may have had in mind the
people of the South who had remained more attached to cattle-

[1] Many people imagine that the honey is fruit honey, but the honey referred to
in the saying, as also in the case of Jacob's gift to Joseph of 'the choice products of
the land' (Genesis 43, 11) can only be a natural product; no saying would make a
land 'overflow' with a cultivated product. From Egyptian sources, we know how
rich Canaan was in bees' honey as early as ibil. 2000 B.C.

breeding than the people of Ephraim. The description of the land
is, however, not the only remnant of the old tradition here. The
prayer begins with the words: *Arammi obed abi*, 'An Aramæan
gone astray was my father'. The alliterative connection of the
three words, the thrice-recurring guttural sound is, as almost
always in the Bible, not incidental and no mere stylistic orna-
ment: the intention is that these words should be impressed upon
the listener or the reader in a particular way; they form a phrase
that is easy to learn by heart. Even at a first hearing the connection with the words that follow appears to be questionable:
'An Aramæan gone astray was my father; and he went down into
Egypt' does not sound like a straightforward narrative. If we
enquire who this 'father' is, it becomes even clearer that different
and disparate material has been combined here. Judging from the
text further on, we are to think of Jacob; it is he who goes down
into Egypt, 'sojourns' there and 'becomes there a nation'—
obviously the reference cannot be to Abraham's short stay in
Egypt. On the other hand, how would Jacob come to be spoken
of as an 'Aramæan gone astray'? The fact that his mother is
the sister of Laban the 'Aramæan' and he is his son-in-law does
not make him his fellow-countryman. And the fact that he spends
more than twenty years of his life far away from his tribe is no
justification for describing him as having 'gone astray.' This
word 'gone astray' is pastoral language. It is used when a sheep
has lost the flock to which it belongs (Jeremiah 50, 6; Ezekiel 34,
4, 16; Psalms 119, 176). 'My people hath been lost sheep; their
shepherds have caused them to go astray, they have turned them
away on the mountains: they have gone from mountain to hill,
they have forgotten their resting place', we read in Jeremiah.
'Their shepherds have caused them to go astray'—in the same
words and with the same meaning, though in quite a different
tone of voice Abraham tells the king of the Philistines about his
life (Genesis 20, 13): 'And it came to pass, when God caused
me to go astray from my father's house . . .' A bad shepherd
causes a sheep to go astray from the flock because he is careless;
Abraham's God, of whom he speaks in the plural in order to
make himself understood to the Philistine, caused him to go astray
from his flock because, he, the good shepherd, was caring for him.
In Haran, in the land of Aram, where the tribe of the Terahites,
Abraham's tribe, had settled, this God had caused him to go

away from his kindred and his father's house 'unto a land that
I will show thee' (12, 1), into this land of Canaan. No matter
whether the Terahites really sprang from the Aramæans, who
had once migrated to Ur, for which there is some evidence, or
whether they were called Aramæans, because they had settled
in 'Paddan Aram': Abraham was in fact a 'lost Aramæan'.
The fact that he is nowhere else described as such, but only as a
Hebrew (14, 13)—the latter is presumably not a tribal designa-
tion but merely signifies membership of the community of the
'travellers' or 'immigrants'—is naturally bound up with the
tradition that Abraham had been fetched by God from his
father's house and brought to Canaan to become the ancestor of
a new people: in the hour of 'going astray' he is still an
Aramæan, in Canaan no longer.

It is impossible to ascertain how the connection of the old
saying with the prayer came about. Jacob's Aramæan sojourn
obviously made it easier to associate the 'Aramæan' with his
name.

The instruction to make a feast of the first-fruits, which follows
the prayer, ends with the order that 'the sojourner that is in your
midst' shall, like the poor Levite also, participate therein. There
is some suggestion of an instruction here, not unlike the one that
is given full expression in another place: your fathers, of whom
you have just spoken, once sojourned in this land; now that you
are its masters, let the strangers that are in your midst participate
without stint in all the delights of the land, in all the good things
that YHVH, thy God, has given thee and thy house.

In order to appreciate the spiritual background of the passage,
however, one must read it in connection with the words of
Jeremiah (2, 3): 'Israel is sacredness unto the Lord, the first-
fruits of his increase'. The world is God's field, the peoples His
plantation, Israel His first-fruits. Just as the tree offers Him, the
giver of the land, the first-fruits every year, so Israel must offer
itself to Him as the first-fruits of His world harvest.

One must not completely spiritualize such a conception and
deprive it of the bodily substance without which the spiritual
content would have no real stability. No symbol has authentic
existence in the spirit if it has no authentic existence in the body.
In order that Israel may become the first-fruits of the divine
harvest, it needs a real land as well as a real people. For this

reason the word of the Lord in Jeremiah introduces the saying thus: 'I remember thee the kindness of thy youth, the love of thy betrothal-time, when thou wentest after me in the wilderness, in the land that is not sown.' That is the historic progress of the people into the land that God has promised and given to it.

Twice seven times the name of God is mentioned in the short passage and nine times with the addition 'thy God'.[1] As has already been shown, this working with numbers on the part of the author or the editor has a didactic purpose. If, repeatedly, at every stage of the action, in every important section of the statement, Yhvh is called 'thy God', if stress is laid, in exactly the same way, on the fact that the sanctuary is His sanctuary, the altar His altar, that He is the God addressed in the prayer, then this is a declaration of faith of decisive importance. For the Canaanite the fertility of the soil is the work of natural gods, of many local Baals or, in the more advanced Phœnician culture, of the 'heavenly' Baal, the result of the sexual associations of water-giving and water-receiving divinities. This conception was not restricted to the religious sphere : it determined the cultivation of the soil itself with its magical and orgiastic sexual customs, it permeated the whole life of the peasant. In view of the influence of these pagan beliefs it was a matter of life or death for the faith of Israel and one that became increasingly serious from the time of the entry into the promised land onwards, to make every citizen absolutely and invincibly certain that the God who gives him the fruit of the land, 'corn, wine and oil' (Hosea 2, 10) is the same God who gave Israel the land. The God of history and the God of nature cannot be separated and the land is the token of their unity. The God who brought Israel into this land, it is even He whose eyes are always upon it 'from the beginning of the year even unto the end of the year' (Deuteronomy 11, 12). The uniformly recurring seasons with their blessings are bound to that unique historical act in which God led the people with whom He had made the covenant into the promised land. The creation itself bears witness to the revelation. The land is its witness.

It is only from early Talmudic times that a description of how the offering of the first-fruits was celebrated has come down to

[1] Hence, to complete the symbolic number, in all probability the strange addition of 'to thy God' in the address to the priest (Deuteronomy 26, 3).

us. The report of the Mishna (Bikkurim III) sounds as though
the intention was to preserve something lost and past for the
memory of future generations. We hear how the people from
the surrounding country come to Jerusalem with the first-fruits,
those living close at hand with fresh fruits, those far away with
dried. In the early morning the procession enters the city, headed
by pipers, then the sacrificial bull with gilded horns, and behind
it the men, bearing baskets filled with fruits and garlanded with
grapes, each according to his wealth, golden baskets, silver baskets
and baskets woven from stripped willow-twigs. The artisans of
Jerusalem come out to meet them, greeting those from each
place in turn : ' Brothers, men from the place of such and such a
name, may you come in peace !' But when they stood by the
temple hill the king himself took his basket on his shoulders and
entered in with them. In the forecourt the Levites sang the verse
from the Psalms : ' I will exalt thee, YHVH, for thou hast
drawn me up '. The verb described the lifting of the bucket from
the well. In the context of the action and the prayer that follows,
which gives thanks for the deliverance from Egypt, the quotation
comes to mean : ' Israel gives thanks to God for raising it from
the well of Egypt into the daylight and freedom of its own land.'

What emerges from the report of the Mishna is the living
unity—from the small peasant and the artisan right up to the
king—of a people experiencing and glorifying the blessings of
Nature as the blessings of History. Thus we appreciate the full
meaning of the passage on the offering of the first-fruits, the
unique document of a unique relationship between a people and a
land.

Man and the Earth

IN POPULAR myths from the Far East and the South Sea
Islands to the innermost interior of the African continent the idea
of a primal relationship between man and the earth constantly
recurs : the gods, so it is believed, form the human race out of clay
or slime ; sometimes, for instance in Babylon, the blood of a slaugh-
tered god is mixed in with the clay. In the Biblical story of the
creation the idea is elaborated in a unique manner : from the
very start the whole destiny of man is indissolubly bound up with
the soil but the converse is likewise true. First there is (Genesis 2,

5) an *Adama*, a fertile earth, but there is no man, no *Adam*, to serve it. God the potter forms man of the dust of the Adama and puts him in the garden the fruit trees of which He causes to grow out of the Adama. And again God forms animals and birds from the Adama and brings them to Adam so that he may give to each its right name. But set thus in the centre of the living world the man and woman are guilty of sin. And now, in Adam's hearing, God curses the Adama: he curses it for the sake of man. Furthermore, Adam learns that when he dies he must return to the earth from which he came. Man and the earth are united one with the other from the beginning and to the very end of time.

We have no certain knowledge of the origin of the words *adam* and *adama*, the first of which the Biblical text evidently derives from the second, although there are no strictly philological grounds either for supporting or contradicting the derivation. The Biblical association of the two probably has its source in the fact that ' the light brown man is formed of the light brown earth into which he is finally dissolved' (in Arabic *adima* means to be brown, reddish-brown, and ' brown-red' will also have been the original meaning of the Hebrew *adom*), but it must also have been the light brown colour 'which gave its name to the fruitful earth, which contrasts in its bright, brownish colours with the sterile grey lime rocks of Turon and Cenoman and the dazzlingly white Senon of the deserts'.[1] But the repeated juxtaposition of the two names in the Biblical narrative is more significant than, for example, the Roman derivation of *homo* from *humus* because man is declared to have been ' born out of the earth'. It is intended to express an existential *communion* of the two, a communion which develops into a special kind of *solidarity*. The earth bears the curse of man's sin, it has to answer for it by bringing forth thorns and thistles instead of healthy and abundant fruits. This is something different from Hesiod's making the earth bear fruits of its own accord in the age of the golden race and only need cultivation in later ages. The Biblical earth has to answer for the offences of man who springs from and is dependent on it. They are bound up with one another for better and for worse, but in such a way that it is man who determines the fate of the

[1] Leonhard Rost, *Die Bezeichnungen für Land und Volk im Alten Testament* (Festschrift Otto Proksch, 1934), p. 126.

earth by his conduct, the fate which in return becomes his own. Certainly only a peasant people can possibly speak in such terms about man and the earth; yet apart from the Israel that settled in Canaan I know of no other peasant people that has in fact spoken in this way.

Another Bible story, that of the Flood, shows, it is true, that not only the Adama as such, but the whole earth has to pay the price of man's offences. In that the earth is filled with man's violence, it becomes 'corrupt' itself (Genesis 6, 11). God looks upon the earth and sees the effect of 'all flesh having corrupted his way upon the earth' : 'the earth itself was corrupt'. (6, 12.) And so he decides to corrupt it, that is, to lay waste the earth that is already inwardly corrupt and hence 'to corrupt all flesh', that is, cause it to perish. (6, 17.) But after the end of the Flood, when he makes a covenant with the survivors, with all living creatures and their seed in the sign of the rainbow, he declares that there shall be no more floods 'to corrupt the earth' (9, 11). Here too all the repetition is intended to impress a basic fact on the mind : the earth is and remains in union with man who has been created to 'replenish' and 'subdue' it (1, 28) but the penalty it has to pay shall never again involve its destruction, the uninterrupted process of the seasons shall not cease (8, 22). Of the four pairs of seasons which are named, pride of place is given to the one that belongs not to the world of nature but to the world of cultivation : seedtime and harvest. To such an extent is the story dominated by the basic outlook of the peasant. And here too we also see that even when the whole earth is being spoken of as in responsible communion with man, ultimately what is meant is the Adama from the curse of which Noah is to cause the human race to recover (5, 29) and as whose 'husbandman' he begins the new work.

The association between man and the earth is expressed differently but possibly even more forcibly when it is a matter not of the earth in general but of the land of Canaan in particular.

The series of prohibitions of sexual abuses in the eighteenth chapter of Leviticus ends with an appeal to the people not to defile themselves with all such abominable customs. 'For in all these the nations are defiled which I cast out before you : and the land is defiled : therefore I did visit the iniquity thereof upon it, and the land itself vomited out her inhabitants . . . that the land spue not you out also when you defile it as it spued out the nations that were before you.' The Canaanite peoples have made not only themselves but also the land with which they were connected unclean, inwardly unclean with their abominable customs and the land was only able to rid itself of this impurity by getting rid of the peoples themselves. The same fate will threaten Israel if it becomes unclean and makes the land with which it has been united, unclean. This is repeated at the end of the corresponding penal code (Lev. 20, 22).

The sinful people 'brings the land into guilt', the land in which it has settled (Deuteronomy 24, 4), that is, it puts into a state of inner decay. This state is described most exactly by the word *chanaf*, that (as we may deduce from the meaning of the Arabic verb *chanifa*, to suffer from a sprained foot) may be understood in the sense of being 'out of joint'. 'Ye shall not put out of joint the land wherein ye are', we read in the injunction not to spare the life of a murderer (Numbers 35, 33), 'for blood, it puts the land out of joint: and the land cannot be cleansed of the blood that is shed therein, but by the blood of him that shed it'. The land has its own natural dispensation and order which it loses through human guilt, and only regains when atonement has been made. 'They say', Jeremiah quotes (3, 1) apparently from an old popular saying, 'shall not that land be greatly put out of joint' (whose people is guilty of sexual offences). And he accuses Israel of having polluted the land through her whoredom (v. 9). 'From the prophets of Israel', he cries over the degenerate prophets, 'is dislocation gone forth into all the land' (23, 15). The same but much stronger language is heard in the mourning for the ravished earth in the great vision of destruction which is included in the Book of Isaiah (ch. 24) in which, however, far more than merely Canaan is implied: 'The earth is put out of joint under the inhabitants thereof, because they have transgressed the instructions, overstepped the law, broken the everlasting covenant. Therefore hath a curse devoured the earth.'

An interpretation based merely on the punishment of a people by a reduction in the yield of its land or something of that kind is quite inadequate to explain such utterances. They are obviously based on the belief in a direct connection between man and the earth, a connection of a cosmically ethical character, in which, however, the ethical element is decisive. Man is subject to the

command of a God who reveals His will to him and he has been
placed in such an intimate relationship with the earth by the
creative act of this same God that his attitude to the divine
ordinance has a direct influence, for good or for evil, on the earth
itself. Israel's passionate relationship to the Adama, in which the
fire of this faith is kindled, influences the description of the way
the earth is conditioned by human actions both in the history
of primitive times and in the proclamation of the divine
Covenant.

The communion between man and the earth demands, however, an honest approach on the part of man to everything connected with the soil, in fact, with farming in general, including
the acquisition of land and the sale of the harvest. Amos closes
his speech against the corn profiteers, who ' make the ephah
small and the shekel great' (Amos 8, 5) by saying that the land
' shall tremble for this and rise up wholly like the Nile stream '
(18, 8). And at the end of his protestation of his integrity Job
speaks of the unjust land-usurper (one thinks of Naboth's vineyard) whose ' land cries against him and the furrows thereof com-
plain' (Job 31, 38). This is more than a mere poetic metaphor :
the image represents a basic belief. In Israel the earth is not
merely, as in all other primitive peoples or peoples that preserve
their primeval energy, a living being, but it is also the partner in
a moral, God-willed and God-guaranteed association.

This is the point of view from which we can best understand
the full meaning of the institution of the Sabbatical year, an
institution, the growth of which is, as a Biblical critic has lately
declared,[1] conceivable in an age ' in which the Israelitish tribes
had not yet entirely abandoned the semi-nomadic existence of
their early period, and had in fact begun to cultivate the soil but
had not yet made agriculture the centre of their economy '. There
are, as is well known, two versions of the regulations governing
the Sabbatical year. The first obviously fragmentary version
(Exodus 23, 10 f.) merely says that every seventh year the tribes'
claim to exclusive enjoyment of the land assigned to them shall
cease and the yield shall be made available to all the hungry as
if the land were the common property of all the inhabitants of
the locality, including, though on a lower level, the beasts of the
field. It is true that the second comprehensive and reasoned

[1] Albrecht Alt, *Die Ursprünge des israelitischen Rechts* (1934), p. 65.

version (Leviticus 25, 2-7) must be regarded, in the verbal form
in which it has come down to us, as a later revision, but its constituent elements can no more be explained as the result of
'theological consistency for its own sake'[1] than those of the first
version, but must be understood as the confluence and elaboration
of old legal traditions. In contrast to the first version, the concept
of the Sabbath, the original substance of which may be regarded
as extremely old, is central.[2] The Sabbatical year is the sabbath
of the land, its 'cessation,' for that is the meaning of the
Sabbath. 'When you come into the land that I shall give you,'
the regulation ordains, 'let the land observe a cessation to
Yнvн.' Just as the people's Sabbath is not a mere rest from work
but a holiday dedicated to God, so the sabbath of the land is
more than mere fallowness. Just as all living beings in the community are liberated from the authority of all except the one
Lord on the Sabbath, so too the land has but one Lord in the
Sabbatical year. It is a 'ritually conceived fallowness'.[3] It can be
said in fact that the idea is that the earth is for a time to be free,
so as not to be subjected to the will of man, but left to its own
nature, to be like no-man's-land.[4]

The essential point, however, is that the repose of the field
signifies a divine repose and its freedom a divine freedom. Resting, being free, desisting from labour is not a negative condition,
it is more than the mere cessation of work and dependence, it is
the state of being taken up into the natural operation of the
divine Covenant. 'In the seventh year' so runs the ordnance,
'let there be a great holiday (*shabbat shabbaton*) for the land, a
holiday for Yнvн.' The twofold dative is unambiguous. By being
made free from the authority of the owners, by giving up its
fruits to all, the land is sanctified afresh with each returning sabbatical year. In the regulations governing the Year of Jubilee
contained in the same passage the prohibition of selling land 'in
perpetuity' and the command to grant a redemption for land
that has been sold, are based on the word of God : 'for the land
is Mine, for ye are strangers and sojourners with Me' (Leviticus
25, 23). The land does not belong to individuals but to all, it is of

[1] Max Weber, *Gesammelte Aufsätze zur Religionssoziologie* (1921), III, pp. 57, 76.
[2] Cf. the survey of research on the subject in Walther Eichrodt, *Theologie des
Alten Testaments*, I (1933), p. 59, note 3.   [3] Alt, loc. cit.
[4] Johannes Pedersen, *Israel, Its Life and Culture*, (1926), I–II p. 480.

the people because it is of God. All displacements of property, all
the latifundia that have developed are compensated for the year
of ' home bringing ', (for that seems to be the meaning of *yobel*),
everything is ' brought home ' into the people's divinely appointed tenure of the land. But the same argument can also be applied
to the Sabbatical year : inasmuch as the produce of the land
is made available to all at regular intervals, the fact that the
land is the Lord's is repeatedly made manifest.

We are also familiar with the sacred relationship between God,
the people and the land from other early theocratic writings,
in particular from ancient Arabian politico-religious documents ;[1]
conquered territory is surrendered to the God and the people,
the tribal God is the owner of all property. But nowhere except
in the holy scriptures of Israel is the socio-religious conclusion
drawn, nowhere else is the dignity of the soil blessed with fertility
raised to the level of the religious ethos inherent in these exacting
demands on the human cultivators of the soil.

The root *shabat* is solemnly repeated seven times in the regulations for the Sabbatical year contained in Leviticus. And it
recurs another seven times in that section of the great warning
(26, 3-45), which is dominated by the theme of the non-
observance of the Sabbatical year (34-43). This passionate
emphasis on numbers is genuinely Biblical and the regular public
reading of the texts will also have impressed it on the feelings of
the listening congregation by means of the rhythmical reiteration.
This theme is decisive in the final climax of the announcement of
punishment.

The presupposition is the land's claim to a Sabbatical year; it
is its due just as it is God's due. What is due to it will be granted
when the people has been driven away from it. ' And I will scatter
you among the heathen, and will draw out a sword after you '
(26, 33). Just as the sword of the cherubs once barred the first
man's return to the lost Paradise, so God Himself here intends
to be the sword-bearing guardian of the promised, imparted and
then forfeited land. The land is to become free at last by being
emptied of human beings. When the people that has refused to
keep the Sabbatical year (we do not know whether it was ever
kept at all in the pre-exilic age), is driven out of its land and
people and land separated from one another, then the land will

[1] Cf. Martin Buber, *Königtum Gottes*, 2nd ed. (1936), pp. 56 ff.

at last receive its due : in other words, the Sabbatical years withheld from it by the people are now to be made up for in a long
uninterrupted time of fallowness. But the curse is not God's final
word, it is superseded by a promise which is nevertheless profoundly interwoven with the curse, in that the association of man
and earth, of people and land is expressed in a memorable and
peculiar fashion by the repetition of one and the same word with
a double meaning. The verb *ratsa,* in the Kal-form, means roughly
'by a service', and, in the Hifil-form, 'to render a valid, satisfac-
tory service '—this verb recurs in various forms and always
strongly emphasized. Thus both the long, unyielding repose of the
land, which makes up for the neglected sabbaths, and the long
and great atonement of the people, which overcomes the tension
between itself and God, because it turns back to Him and
' its heart humbles itself ' (26, 41)—both are covered by the same
word and thus maintained in a firm mutual relationship. In the
period in which Israel is in the land of its enemies, the land shall
be satisfied by its sabbaths, it will receive all that is due to it,
' as long as it lieth desolate it shall rest, the time it did not rest
in your sabbaths, when ye dwelt upon it ' (26, 35); (the verbal
play on *beshabtotekhem* ' in your sabbaths ' and *beshibtkhem*
' when ye dwelt—' is in fact more than a mere play on words).
But as both the Sabbatical year and the Sabbath, indeed all ' cessation ', is consecrated to YHVH, what the land receives with this
long holiday is at the same time something that it fulfils, that it
fulfils to God : it ' satisfies ' Him, paying off His Sabbaths.

Likewise the offences of the people are ' satisfied ' by its pen-
ance, and it receives the expiation of its guilt by turning back to
God. Thus the one verb prepares the way for the restoration of
the disturbed relationship between God, the people and the land.
The 'satisfaction' (*ratson*), the grace of God which exists between
Him, the people and the land exceeds the strictly legal settlement
of accounts.

Three verses from the end of the 2nd Book of Chronicles (36,
21), the words ' until the land has satisfied (paying off) its sabbaths ', are put into the mouth of the prophet Jeremiah as if they
had already been fulfilled. ' For as long as it lay desolate is kept
sabbath, to fulfil seventy years ' are the words that follow. A
proclamation of Cyrus calling on Israel to return from Babel into
the land is quoted as the fulfilment of the ' word of the Lord

spoken by the mouth of Jeremiah'. The final words of the proclamation are also the conclusion of the Hebrew Bible: 'Who
there is, among ye of all his people, the Lord his God with him,
he shall go up' (the same words appear in the more detailed
version of the call at the beginning of the book of Ezra). This
last sentence sounds like an historical profession of faith in the
intimate relationship between God, the people and the land.

THE PROMISE

TO HAVE experienced the eternal blessing of the earth as an
historical blessing, and to have introduced the solidarity between
man and the earth as an eternal instruction into the historical
foundations of a people—we have seen that this is the all-
important particularity in Israel's relationship to its own land.
This relationship is, on the one hand, an absolute one, but on the
other, an historically established relationship. Absoluteness and
historicity seem to be mutually exclusive; where they are fused
in a people's faith, a reality of the spirit arises, which, as we know
from the message of the Bible, carries the breath of the Absolute
far into the future history of the human race. Such a fusion of the
Absolute and the historical took place in the relationship between
Israel and its land in the event known to the faithful as the
Promise.

The Promise means that within history an absolute relationship
between a people and a land has been taken into the covenant
between God and the people.

Some peoples have preserved and shaped the traditions of
early tribal wanderings in legends. Occasionally the legends tell
of gods helping the tribe on its journeyings and afterwards assist-
ing with the building of its settlement. But I know of no other
occasion in the wide ranges of the history of religion when a god
'gives' a land to a people, and of no words comparable to the
following (Genesis 12, 7): 'Unto thy seed will I give this land.'
This simple element has not been found anywhere else in the
whole history of comparative religion and it looks to me as if it
is in fact quite unique. We know a good deal about the forms
assumed by inter-tribal covenants, especially among the Semitic

tribes, and there are also reports of covenants being made between gods and men; here and there we are reminded of Biblical characteristics, but the content of the covenant which the Bible authenticates is unique, and the giving of the land is an essential constituent.

The Biblical belief that the land is a divine gift must not be taken as meaning that the God of this particular faith gave a land to one people only. When Amos reminds the people (9, 7) that the Lord not only brought up Israel out of Egypt but also the Philistines and Aramæans out of their former habitations into their present domains, the form in which he does so ('Is it not so . . . ?') suggests that his intention is not to proclaim a new doctrine but to make the people fully aware of a traditional one; on the other hand, however, he does hint that only in the case of Israel has the relation of the giver to the receiver developed into one of 'knowledge', of election, revelation and covenant: the other peoples led by God which have received a land from Him do not know His true name, His nature, His universality and His claim; each of them knows only that their god, the tribal god, led them into this land and presented it to them. The diplomatic style of Jephthah's message to the king of a neighbouring land is to be considered thus (Judges 11, 24): what he demands of him is not the acknowledgement of YHVH as the one true god but merely recognition of the gift of land by God to Israel on the basis of reciprocity. Nevertheless his own faith in the one common deliverer, leader and leige lord of the peoples, is not concealed: if you refuse, so the message continues, to stand on the basis of mutual acknowledgment, then (11, 27) 'the Lord *the Judge* shall judge this day between the children of Israel and the children of Ammon!' In the middle of a political-historical treatise this comes very close to that most comprehensive saying of all in which (Genesis 18, 25) Abraham calls his God 'the Judge of all the earth'.

Israel—this is the heart of its relationship to its own early history and indeed the heart of its whole historical faith—is the one people that knows the truth how it came into possession of its land. Among all the traditions of the world this is the only one that tells of the promise of a land to a people.

The man Abraham appears in the Scriptures as the earliest recipient of this Promise. If we examine the scanty accounts of

his life before the Promise we discover first of all that he is a
wanderer; apart from the genealogical names and dates we learn
nothing more than the stages of his journeyings. The information
is, however, not inconsiderable. He wanders with his kith and kin
and with their herds—not the camel herds of the Bedouin, but
the mixed herds of the semi-nomad of a high grade—from Ur,
by which is obviously meant the recently excavated south Babylonian city, on the great north-west caravan route 'to go into the
land of Canaan' (Genesis 11, 31). Probably Ur was not the
native place of the family, probably they came from the
Aramæan north and moved from there to Ur, thus returning to
their home territory when they came on their wanderings to
Haran. There they settled. They did not move on any further.
Did they in fact intend to go to Canaan and did they give up
their intention, possibly because Haran unexpectedly fulfilled the
purpose of their journeyings—whether economic, political,
religious, or a mixture of some kind? In any case they feel probably afresh that the Aramæan land is 'their land' (12, 1). And
now Abraham, with his companions, parts from his kindred and
goes forth into the land of Canaan, and so—according to the
Bible—to the original target of his wanderings because a God,
whom the chronicler calls YHVH bids him do so. We are not told
when Abraham actually learns the name of this God which he
begins, soon afterwards, to call out over the altars which he
builds in Canaan (12, 8). We are not even told whether He was
already his god before He gave him the command. There is a
hint, however, in another chapter of the story (15, 7) that it was
this God who had brought him out of Ur 'to give him this land
to inherit it'. But we do not know whether to take this as meaning that a manifestation similar to that which followed in Haran
had already been given to Abraham in Ur—this is hardly prob-
able, since it was not for Abraham, but for his father Terah to
make the decision—or merely that Terah received an inspiration
the divine origin of which he did not know, but which he simply
ascribed to his own god. A manifestation to Terah or to him and
his kindred can hardly be meant (although the apocryphal book
of Judith which probably dates from the Maccabean age, seems
to hint (5, 7) at something of the kind: ' ... that they served
the one God of heaven, who commanded them to move on and
settle in Haran' as the call which came in Haran refers un-

mistakably to a renunciation by Abraham of his father's house
for religious reasons ('Get thee out of thy country, and from thy
kindred and from thy father's house'). A tradition preserved in
a passage in the book of Joshua (24, 2), which cannot, however,
be considered of an early date, explicitly makes Terah, who is
said to have dwelt 'across the river' i.e. east of the River
Euphrates, 'serve other gods'. We are not told here or anywhere
else what kind of gods. But we know that the holy city of Ur was
the centre of the worship of the moon and that Haran was its
second main centre, probably founded by moon-worshipping
semi-nomads who had come from the region of Ur. The moon
god was in fact the god of the nomads and the travellers, the god
of the caravans. He obviously is the god whom Abraham renounces when he entrusts himself to the guidance of YHVH. The
difference between the leadership of the former and that of the
latter god is not merely that the guidance of the moon god is
limited to clear nights, whereas that of YHVH is unlimited, but
also that the moon god merely guides and guards travellers on
the way to destinations determined by themselves, whereas
YHVH Himself determines the goal of their journey. He takes the
initiative, He 'leads out', He brings them 'into a land which
He shows unto them'. Once again we are confronted with a
phenomenon unique and unparalleled in the history of human
religion.

In the story of Abraham's journey from Haran to Canaan and
his first excursions in the land (Genesis 12, 1-9) the method of
drawing attention to the crucial points by repetition again predominates: the essential word 'land' recurs seven times and
'Canaan' three times. This would be incomprehensible if this
were merely a report, but the report is full of prophecy. It must
be noted that God's first call to Abraham (12, 2 f.) already
contains a great promise but not yet the promise of the land.
This is first given not in Haran but in Canaan itself (v.7)—only
when God can say to His chosen one: 'Unto thy seed will I give
this land'. In the original promise of the land it is not any land,
not a 'good' land, but this land here that God shows to Abraham.
In Haran God bids His chosen one go into the land 'that I will
let thee see'. In Shechem he sees it—and it is here for the first
time that God allows Himself to be 'seen' (v.7). In Haran he
merely 'speaks' to him; it is not until he reaches Canaan that we

hear of that standing face to face before God which the Bible calls the ' seeing ' of God and this is the first place where we hear of it : the man to whom God gives to see the land is the first to see God Himself.

It is fundamentally important that the man should now roam through the land and see it with his own eyes, for it is 'this' land that the Lord has promised to show him. God not merely brings him into it, He leads him ' throughout all the land of Canaan ' (Joshua 24, 3). After the separation from Lot, that is from that part of the company which is to mingle with the Canaanites, God bids him (Genesis 13, 14) look into all directions and then to walk about in the land ' in the length of it and in the breadth of it ', so that he may become familiar with the land that is to be his, namely the ' whole land ', for the Promise is now changed in this form. In this story too (ch. 13) the word *erets*, earth recurs nine times. The dust of the *erets*, the dust of the earth is deliberately chosen here as a simile for the increase of the people (' I will make thy seed as the dust of the earth : so that if a man can number the dust of the earth, then shall thy seed also be numbered '). Only in association with this earth and with this land can the people be what they are meant to be : ' a blessing ' (12, 2).

The confirmation and renewal of the Promise which is promulgated to the people in Egypt and at the Exodus after the appointed centuries is in quite a different language altogether. Instead of the frequent repetitions of the word ' land ' hammering into the listener or reader that ' this is the main point ', we have the confrontation of two ' lands ' (Exodus 3, 8 : 33, 1), the land of affliction and the land of the Promise. God ' went down ' to ' bring the people up out of that land into a good and large land ', into a pleasant and free land. He brings them forth out of the land of Egypt to the land that He swore to their fathers. This oath is the constant background of what is said. The groaning of the children of Israel in Egypt makes God ' remember ' the covenant which He made with their forefathers (6, 5), the content of which is described (6, 4) as ' to give them the land of Canaan, the land of their sojournment, wherein they had sojourned '. The God who ' remembers ' the covenant stirs the memory of the people. The land to which they have been brought is not simply a land chosen at random for its fertility ; it is the land to which they are bound by the tradition of their fathers' life. Remember : the fathers told our fathers of the good and the large land. Aforetime, God led first the forefather into the length and breadth of the land and let him gaze at it to his heart's content so that his faith might become assured and be handed on to his children ; now the word of the Lord recalls it to the memory of the children's children, that their spirit may see the unseen land and urge them through the wilderness to take it in possession.

They go, with the image of the land within them. Why does God now bid them, so near to their goal, send out spies instead of letting them learn from the lips of Moses what they need to know about the land ? The questions go so far as to inquire (Numbers 13, 19) whether the land, this same land whose goodness has been praised so many times, is good or bad, fat or lean. What is meant is that the place of the wavering vision, woven from grandmothers' tales, is now to be taken by the eye-witness account, and by contact with a beautiful though hard and stern reality based on the direct experience of those commissioned to spy out the land. They confirm the stories of the fertility of the land but these seven good words are followed by seventy evil words;[1] they depict the might of the natives in bold colours and give warning that it is a land ' that eateth up the inhabitants thereof ' (v. 32) as a hostile land eats up its prisoners of war (Leviticus 26, 38). The Bible does not interpret the terrible statement as an untruth; even in the Babylonian exile Ezekiel (36, 13 f.) in God's name declares that from the hour in which Israel is allowed to return home into its own land, the ' land shall devour men no more '. Whether the land devours its inhabitants depends on themselves : those who rebel against the Lord, from them is their protecting ' shadow ' (Numbers 14, 9) departed, whereas those in whom the Lord delights are superior to all danger; if Israel does not acknowledge this it rebels against God. Because it rebels against Him the people must turn back into the desert (14, 25), even though so near its goal, by way of the Red Sea, so to say in the direction of Egypt. The ' forty years ' (14, 33 f.) of wandering follow.

At the end of these wanderings, in the plains of Moab, on the east side of Jordan (Deuteronomy 1, 5, cf. Numbers 22, 1) after

---

[1] More accurately seventy-one, but the first word is merely a conjunction between the two sections.

they had taken forty years to make the eleven days' journey from
Mount Sinai thus far, in sight of the promised land, the history
of the Promise as described in the Bible enters a new phase to fit
the new situation. In Moses' great survey of the past and glance
into the future, composed with true Biblical wisdom, from ancient
remnants of tradition and elaborations of a later age practised
in the art of formulation and preaching, as a book on its own, the
land is spoken of in a new way, a third way. It is no longer com-
mitted to inner vision, no longer remembered and glorified from
a distance; it lies 'before thee' and the cry is heard: 'Go up,
inherit!' (Deuteronomy 1, 21). It is true that its gifts are praised
once more and more concretely and impressively than ever before
(8, 7–10): 'thou shalt not lack any thing in it'. The new thing,
however, that was not allowed to appear in earlier times and now
had to appear, is that its secret is revealed (11, 10–17). Of all
lands this is the one which is by its very nature in a special way
subject to and dependent on the providence and grace of God.
To make this knowledge the possession of the people's hearts,
the two lands, Egypt and Canaan, the land 'whence ye have
come' and 'the land to which thou comest to inherit it', must
once again confront each other. But now it is more than the
mere comparison of two different situations of the people. The
natural character of the two countries is compared, the contrast
being intended to bring out the nature of Canaan with absolute
clarity. Egypt's fertility does not depend on the changing gifts of
heaven which it receives in extremely scanty measure; Creation
has provided for it once and for all, the Nile has been created to
flood the land every year, its strength is irregular, it is true, but,
by an enormous technical effort of the whole population from
the earliest times men have improved the work of Creation by
erecting dams and sluices to regulate the current, by digging
channels and ditches to distribute the water and by building
water wheels to raise it from the river and lakes and convey it
into the channels and ditches: thou canst 'water this land with
thy food, like a garden of herbs' (Deuteronomy 11, 10). Canaan
is quite different. Certainly it is 'a land of brooks of water, of
fountains, and depths that spring out of valleys and hills'
(Deuteronomy 8, 7) but all this comes and goes, the land is
insecure, 'it drinketh water of the rain of heaven' (11, 11), it
is in the hand of God who 'visits' it again and again, 'the

eyes of Y<small>HVH</small> thy God are always upon it, from the beginning
of the year even unto the end of the year' (11, 12). This is the
place where grace rules for all to see. What it expects from man,
from the people is 'love' (11, 13). To an Israel that loves him
Y<small>HVH</small> 'will give the rain of your land in his due season, the
autumn soaker and the spring shower' (11, 14), but to an Israel
that ' turns aside and serves other gods ' (11, 16) ' he shuts up the
heaven that there be no rain and that the land yield not her
fruit ' (11, 17). The historical books of the Bible provide a great
example of this in the story of Elijah (1 Kings, ch. 18) who, in
the drought and famine that last for many years, reproves the
people that they incline ' to hop on two boughs at once ', instead
of deciding between Y<small>HVH</small> and Baal: though chastisement
God turns the heart of Israel (18, 37) and the rain comes that
had been withheld for so long.

The Bible does not mean at all, of course, that Egypt was
abandoned by God to the whims of nature, and withdrawn from
His direct influence. The Nile, like the whole world, is in God's
hands. That is plainly proclaimed both in the story of the great
famine in the days of Joseph and in that of the plague of blood
in the days of Moses. The prophets declare how Y<small>HVH</small> dries up
the rivers of Egypt (Isaiah 19, 6 ff.) but all this is as it were the
result of an abnormal action on the part of the Godhead, whereas
the very nature of the land of Canaan bears witness to the un-
remitting providence of God. And it is its nature that qualifies it
to be the pledge of the covenant.

Herodotus tells (2, 12 f.) how the Egyptian priests with whom
he had spoken, compared their land with Greece. They gave him
to understand that the Greeks, who were dependent on rain,
were subject to the arbitrariness of Zeus, whereas Egypt had been
quite independent of the changes and chances of the divine Providence from time immemorial. If the statement quoted is based
on a fundamental Egyptian point of view (and there is some
reason for assuming that it is) it may be regarded as the background of the saying in Deuteronomy. Egypt did in fact ' breed
a tribe of gods unrelated to the climatic conditions of the
Mediterranean region '.[1] As far as water is concerned the Egyptian feels himself independent of the gods in all concerns of agri-

---

[1] Ellen Churchill Semple, *The Geography of the Mediterranean Region* (1932),
p. 511.

culture and the soil; he has, as it were, a contract with nature and does not need to trouble the higher powers with his fears and hopes. The priests who spoke to Herodotus regard that as a great advantage. The Bible, on the other hand, considers this being provided for as seriously prejudicial to the kind of life that really matters: the life of intercourse with a wrathful and merciful Godhead. In Egypt Israel was merely involved in the natural processes of existence; by bringing it to Canaan, to the land which is the object of His immediate personal care, God sets it into direct relationship with Himself. The rhythm of the unfolding seasons is punctuated by a mighty progression of success and failure: fear of the divine wrath and the struggle to merit His favour are followed by the lifting of the eyes to Him.

From this point a direct line can be traced to the summits of Israel's faith: to the trust in ' the God that hideth himself ' (Isaiah 45, 15). The genuine life of faith develops on the spiritual heights, but it springs from the depths of the distress of the earthbound body. The Israelite praying for rain for his thirsty land is the man who will be praying later on for redemption. It is not for nothing that the great prophets of the Bible, from Amos (8, 11) who prophesies the destruction of the northern kingdom, to the nameless prophet (Isaiah 44, 3) who proclaims the return from the Babylonian exile, establish a close relationship between the thirst for water and the thirst for the Word of God, between the outpouring of the water and the outpouring of God's spirit. This is far more than a poetic metaphor, more even than a symbolic concept. It is an essential element of the Faith. If we examine all the passages, in which ' Deutero-Isaiah ' glorifies water as a miraculous gift, in the light of his message, we shall recognize the religious insight which links them all: wherever the action of nature as well as spirit is perceived as a gift, Revelation takes place. In its inmost essence nature is not an incessantly turning wheel and the spirit is not the fruit of human development: both are the gestures of one hand. ' For I will pour water upon him that is thirsty, and floods upon the dry ground: I will pour my Spirit upon thy seed, and my blessing upon thine offspring.'

The land of the Promise plays a great part in the growth of this faith. Of course here too, there are ' times and seasons ', here as on the whole earth, Yoreh the former rain and Malkosh the latter rain in their due season. In the same speech of Moses in which he compares Egypt and Canaan, those who love God are assured that God will 'give them the rain of their land in his due season, the former rain, and the latter rain.' But in spite of the fixed seasons, the rain are variable. In Canaan Israel realizes that rain is a *gift* and it recognizes the Giver.

Not all ears, however, are ready to accept the teaching of this land. In this same land the Semitic tribes that settled in it before Israel, and perhaps even those that were there before them, saw in the waters of the sky and earth the outpouring of the ' Baalim ' who mate with the goddesses of the soil. They succeeded in passing on this idea and the rites appertaining to it to an apparently not small part of the Israelite newcomers, and in Israel they knew how to reconcile the service of the leader god YHVH, which they retained, with that of all the swarming fertility spirits. To be sure, it was the Lord who had brought Israel to the land, but it was obviously the 'masters' or 'owners' or ' husbands' (all that is implied in the name of Baal) of the land who made it fruitful. In the struggle between the exclusive belief in YHVH and the mixed-up religion whose adherents wish to hop on two boughs at once, like a bird alighting on a forked branch, Elijah achieves the decisive victory inasmuch as the people worship and call on YHVH as ' *the godhead*,' that is, the only godhead : all the blessings of Nature are not the product of Baalite pairings, but the gift of the one God YHVH. Yet a mere century later, shortly before the destruction of the Northern Kingdom, Hosea (2, 10–15) has to remind the people that it is YHVH and not the Baalim who gives the corn, wine and oil, and that He can therefore also *take away* each of them ' in its due season '. This is the teaching that ripened in Canaan out of the meeting of this land with this people—not all at once, but through a long process of growth in which all the obstacles were overcome. A faith like this, much as it is a revealed faith, does not drop ready-made from the sky. A definite, uniquely constituted plot of land and a definite, uniquely constituted kind of man—both are needed to develop it.

' In the whole Aegean world primitive religion was bound up in the needs of tillage; the supreme god was he who sent the beneficent rains upon the thirsting fields '.[1] Zeus too is a giver of rain. From the peaks of his holy mountains he moves the

[1] Semple, loc. cit., p. 513.

thick clouds (Iliad 16, 297). He is invoked, in the words of the
prayer quoted by Marcus Aurelius, to rain on the cornlands and
pastures of the Athenians. Drought-ridden Attica regarded itself
as especially dependent on his help and on the Acropolis a statue
of the earth supplicated Zeus for rain. As in the Baalite world of
thought, so here the granting of its request was interpreted as a
fertilization of the earth. But in Greece power over the heavenly
waters is never seen in connection with the mutual relationship
between the god and his people as it is in Israel. The Greeks,
it is true, have their own story of the Flood in which Zeus sends
down great showers of rain from heaven which inundate the
black earth and destroy all but a few men (according to Plato's
account, Solon is supposed to have heard, again from an Egyptian
priest, that this divine cleansing of the earth had been carried
out in every country except Egypt where, even during such flood-
times, only the annual overflowing of the Nile took place, for
'so it is decreed'); but it is difficult to imagine the matter coming
to a head in the Greek domains after the manner of the covenant
which the Biblical god makes with the earth in the sign of the
rainbow. To be sure, according to Homer, with his rainfloods
Zeus helps other gods hurl down the ship's wall built without the
statutory offerings; but such an act as that of YHVH who, to
lead the battle lines of Israel, marches out of the fields of Edom
over the trembling earth, makes the clouds drop water and the
rivers flood, and puts to rout the enemy's chariots (Judges 4,
14 f.; 5, 4, 26) is fundamentally foreign to him. What differentiates YHVH in such cases from all Zeus-like beings is that
which makes it impossible for Him to be surrounded by a Pan-
theon even in early days Israel learns to know Him as the God
that leads the family and the tribe from land to land, as the God
who makes the covenant with the elect, who then, renewing the
covenant with the people, leads it into 'this land' and again
marches at the head of its liberation journeys. In this His uniqueness is implied from of old. He is the leader and He makes the
covenant. From this He is known—though of all the Semitic
tribes which believed in tribal gods, only Israel achieves this
knowledge—as the god who makes a covenant with His creation
and leads mankind to redemption. When men heard of His
leadership they felt that even the stars were His servants. ('They
fought from heaven; the stars in their courses fought against

Sisera' (5, 20). Even before the Promise is fulfilled He shows the stars like crown jewels (Genesis 15, 5) and solemnly takes the little land of Canaan into His possession.

Of Abraham the Bible relates that after 'this land' had been promised to him he built altars in the north and 'called out the name of the Lord' (Genesis 12, 8; 13, 4); much later, after he had been given the promised son, Abraham planted a grove in the south and 'called there on the name of the Lord' (21, 33). This 'calling on the name of the Lord' is to be understood neither as a prayer nor as a sermon to the heathen, but as proclamation. In the same way the name of the conqueror is called on a conquered city (2 Samuel, 12, 28), and the names of the owners on landed property (Psalm 49, 12). Abraham 'walks before the Lord' (Genesis 17, 1) as a herald before his God, who will one day enter this land with the people of the Promise, and he takes hold of the land for His sake by calling out His name. To be sure, the whole earth is His but just as He desires to make Israel His own 'peculiar treasure', so in a special way He lays hold of Canaan, when He promises it to Israel. The word of God that says of the earth is His, but just as He desires to make Israel His own another saying 'for the land is mine' which refers to Canaan (Leviticus 25, 23), but the following clause 'for ye are strangers and sojourners with me' clearly affirms the special character of this possession.

He who brings, as we heard from Amos, all wandering, land-seeking peoples into their new dwelling places, has set 'strangers and sojourners with himself' only in this one place, strangers and sojourners who are to be directly obedient to Him (*kohanim* (Exodus 19, 6), the original meaning of which is not priests but a kind of adjutants). This is closely connected with the fact that He has always made this land the particular object of His personal care, the land that He visits and which is ever before His eyes. And, in return, Israel comes to acknowledge Him as the Lord of the whole world precisely because it has acknowledged Him in this special manner as the Lord of the land. It comes to understand the Promise as an act of election on the part of the Almighty who chooses for Himself one people out of all the peoples and one land out of all lands and brings them together in order to establish an outpost of His Kingdom.

Nevertheless, the covenant between God, people and land that

is thus established, is broken by the people. But it has not come
to an end, nor shall it do so. The prophets may upbraid the
people violently but the nearer the State approaches to collapse
the more clearly do they insist that the Promise made to the
fathers, that Israel should dwell ' in this place ', was given ' for
ever and ever ' (Jeremiah 7, 7). In years to come, when Israel
purifies itself, God will restore the people (33, 7) and restore the
land (33, 11), both of them together. He will ' plant them in this
land assuredly with His whole heart and with His whole soul '
(32, 41), that is to say, for ever. The Lord punishes, He
scatters the people in hostile lands and lets the land be devastated
but He forsakes neither the people nor the land, He remains
faithful to the work of his election until the hour of His Kingdom
comes, when it will be laid upon both of them, the people and
the land, to accomplish what was appointed for them aforetime
in the hour of the Promise.

This perfect, ' faithful faithfulness ' (Isaiah 25, 1), with which
YHVH keeps to His Promise and to the Election contained therein,
differentiates Him absolutely from Zeus on account of whose
arbitrary dictates the Egyptian priests condoled the people of
Herodotus and from all his kind. In the language of the Bible
men's trust in Him, their faith, in that undogmatic sense which is
the only one the Bible knows. To trust in the faithfulness of God
this same word emuna denotes both the faithfulness of God and
when it is beyond human understanding—for it is indeed beyond
human understanding—, that is the human emuna that
Abraham, the recipient of the Promise, makes true in the face
of the incomprehensible Promise (Genesis 15, 6 : ' And he trusted
in the Lord '). For this reason Paul praises him as the father of
the faithful ; but he is merely the father of the ' trustful '; Paul
found the ' faith' that can be formulated dogmatically in the
descendants of the worshippers of Zeus. The eternal meaning of
the Promise ' of this land ' is grounded in the mutual relationship
between emuna and emuna, between God's faithfulness and the
people's trust.

The Redemption

WE FIND in many peoples of antiquity, and also in Talmudic
and post-Talmudic Jewry, the conception of a holy place as the

centre of the earth, its 'navel'. Apart from a few isolated hints
(Ezekiel 38, 12) no evidence of such an idea has come down to us
from the Bible, and certainly none that might suggest the site
of the Temple in Jerusalem. On the other hand, however, we
observe how, in the prophetic writings, an image of Zion as
the centre of the future, redeemed world is gradually established.
This image is peculiar to the prophetic literature of Israel and
the Psalms which derive from it; as far as I know there is
nothing analogous anywhere else in the sacred books of the
peoples. But it is particularly the book of Isaiah in which the
image is fully developed. To see this clearly, however, one must
rid oneself of the familiar idea that speeches, songs and sayings
of the prophet Isaiah are combined in this book with later
material which is foreign to him and was associated with the
earlier material for purely technical reasons. With a few excep-
tions the contents of the book are indeed connected with Isaiah;
in other words, apart from what has been preserved of his own
utterances, it contains the words of disciples of his, in the main
not those who had actually sat at his feet but who adopted his
teaching a long time after his death and elaborated some point
or other in it. Towards the end of the Babylonian exile the most
prominent among them is that mysterious man whose real name
has no more come down to us than that of the other followers of
Isaiah and who is usually called 'Deutero-Isaiah.' Independent
as he is—far and away the most independent figure among the
prophets of the Exile and after the Exile—all the same he deliberately and emphatically models himself on Isaiah as far as the
form and language of his prophecies are concerned, and he wishes
to be considered Isaiah's posthumous disciple, the interpreter and
perfecter of his teaching, as is obvious from a number of unmistakable references.[1] This peculiar relationship between a son
of the Crisis and the master of the high age of Prophecy is shown
particularly clearly in the way in which he elaborates Isaiah's
doctrine of Zion as the eschatological centre of the world.

Of all the prophets of Israel, Isaiah is the only one whose vision
and prophecy are focused on the Temple of Solomon. It was in
the Temple that he had been consecrated a prophet and, in the
vision, he had seen the earthly sanctuary become transformed
into the heavenly. From that hour he knew that this place was

[1] For more details see the last chapter of my book, *The Prophetic Faith* (1949).

chosen to become the centre of the world of God, of God's world-
embracing Kingdom. But it has not yet become that which it has
been chosen to become, because the people of Israel that is to
build this centre by subjecting the whole of its life to the rule of
God, desecrates the sanctuary in which it treads (1, 12) by its
iniquity. It must purify itself and learn righteousness, it must
learn to walk in the light of God (2, 5) before the holy mountain,
now superior to all the mountains of the world, is 'ready' (2, 2)
to receive the delegates of all peoples who will come to share in
the Revelation which shall bring all strife to an end and create
a united humanity. This is the second Revelation, the second
'Tora' (2, 3): the first was given to the people of Israel from
the mountain in the wilderness, the second is now given to the
whole human race from the mountain of the Temple. (Hence the
promise, in a fragment (4, 5) which perhaps does not come from
Isaiah but was certainly written in his spirit, that the cloud of
smoke and a flaming fire will stand over it as once over Sinai.)
Here, when all evil has been rooted out, will be the centre of a
peaceful intercourse of the nations (11, 6–8 represented symbolically as animals) in mutual goodwill and trust. ' In that day
shall Israel be the third with Egypt and Assyria '—the two world
powers which have waged war on each other and on Israel for so
long—as a no less important ' third power ', ' a blessing in the
midst of the land' (19, 24).

This is the context in which Isaiah's teaching on the *security*
of Zion is to be understood. Because it is destined to be the centre
of the Kingdom of God, thus the prophet declares, no earthly
power can do it any harm. Therefore the Assyrians and their
auxiliary troops, the ' throng' of all the nations that fight against
mount Zion ' (29, 8), shall be scattered as chaff : God Himself,
' YHVH of hosts ', will come down ' to fight for mount Zion '
(31, 4)—the same verb is deliberately used here, in a sense that is
otherwise quite unusual, to describe the action of God and of
the enemy. And there as here Zion is called ' the hearth of God ';
this refers of course to the sacrificial rites, but, for Isaiah, the
altar fire of the Temple is fundamentally different from all other
sacrificial fires of the peoples, a token of the presence of the
' King ' (6, 5) and of that divine dominion over all the world
which will move to its consummation from this place.

The danger of this teaching, the fact that it is apt to produce a false sense of security in the people, which may work against the prophetic call to purification, is realized by the line of prophets from Micah—perhaps a rebellious disciple of Isaiah—to Jeremiah. They do their very utmost to strike the hearts of the careless people who make the existence of the sanctuary an excuse for their evasion of the divine challenge: they prophesy the destruction of the Temple. Fourteen years after the fulfilment of this prophecy, Ezekiel plans the building of the new temple; but there is no sign in his writing of the templocentric view according to which the sanctuary in Jerusalem is the centre of the redeemed earth of the future. Nevertheless in the hours of the Catastrophe and those that follow it a new elaboration of Isaiah's view is prepared, the essential statements of which have, quite logically, been incorporated into the Book of Isaiah, which we may thus regard as the templocentric book *par excellence* in the corpus of Israelite prophecy.

The first of these statements is contained in the small collection of fragments (chs. 24–27) consisting chiefly of pieces which come, in my opinion, from the last phase of the Catastrophe and the early period of the Exile. Here it is proclaimed (24, 23) that ' YHVH of hosts shall reign in mount Zion '. It is a reign over all people and ' in this mountain shall YHVH of hosts make unto all people a feast ' (25, 6), a homage feast: it is repeated three times that the invitation and the consolations of God ' which shall wipe away the tear from off all faces ' apply to all peoples. Just as the veil of sorrow which God lifts from the faces of all peoples probably does not signify the sadness of the single person but the sufferings which arise from the conflicts of the peoples, so the mysterious ' swallowing up of death for ever ' (25, 8) seems to refer not to the bestowal of immortality on the single person but to the overcoming of the power of death that governs the relationships between the peoples. No less mysterious, however, is the taking away of the ' reproach of his people ' from ' all the earth '. In this context Israel, of which one naturally tends to think here, can hardly be meant. If we compare this statement with the cognate 47th Psalm, one of those in which the accession of God as king over ' the peoples ' is glorified, we see that ' the noble men of the peoples ' who gather around the ' throne of His holiness '—probably mount Zion is meant here too—are conjointly called ' the people of the God of Abraham ', because he.

' the father of the multitude of the peoples ' (a phrase that is
certainly not meant to be taken genealogically) is the one in whom
' all the clans of the earth shall bless themselves'. Thus the
words of Isaiah may also refer to the human people gathered
together from all the peoples of the earth whose 'reproach',
namely the disintegration into hostile, mutually foreign peoples
that originated in the tower of Babel, is now removed from the
whole earth. Here Isaiah's prophecy of the peoples streaming to
the mountain (to which the final words 'for the Lord hath
spoken it' probably refer) seems to have been elaborated into a
new and uniform image of the divine King, who on His mountain throne wipes away the tears from all His peoples as a father
wipes them from the faces of all his children and thus redeems
them, through the followship of His table and His hand, from
the common reproach.

The transformation of Isaiah's Zionistic outlook by 'Deutero-
Isaiah' and his school, which begins in the late period of the
Exile, is far more comprehensive and far-reaching. The hour that
is proclaimed here is that in which God returns to Zion to begin
His reign as King (52, 7). The reign of the one great Messianic
peace that now begins is described in pictures that readopt the
motifs of Isaiah, partly using the same words as when (65, 25)
the prophecy of the mutual understanding of wild and tame
animals—in this context they are probably intended to be taken
as animals and not as symbols of peoples—ends, like that of
Isaiah, with the words : ' they shall not hurt nor destroy in all
my holy mountain', but something new is added, namely, the
characterization of the hour announced by the prophet as a
moment of world-historical importance. This is only what we
should expect from the prophet who first welcomes Cyrus as the
liberator of both Israel and the enslaved nations and then, when
he is disappointed by him, assigns the task of not merely bringing
Israel back into its own land, but of being a light of the nations
(42, 6; 49, 6) and of 'bringing them that sit in darkness out of
the prison house' (42, 7; 49, 9), to ' the servant of the Lord '
coming from Israel. He, the servant, is to 'make them possess
the desolate possessions' (49, 8), just as Israel, returning from
Babel, is now restored to the possession of its land.

Through this work of liberating and restoring humanity around
the liberation and restoration of Israel the servant becomes the

'covenant of the people': through him the peoples are bound together into one people, in him the people compounded of the peoples is represented. And through him redeemed Zion becomes the centre of the redeemed world. The redemption is valid, however, not only for humanity but for the whole world, and it is precisely this world-redemption that is centred in Zion. At one and the same time God 'plants' the heaven and says to Zion, 'Thou are my people' (51, 16); at one and the same time He creates a new heaven and a new earth and 'creates' Jerusalem (65, 17 f.). The renewal of the world and the renewal of Zion are one and the same thing, for Zion is the heart of the renewed world. Isaiah's Zionocentric view has here acquired cosmic proportions.

The people of Israel is called upon to be the herald and pioneer of the redeemed world, the land of Israel to be its centre and the throne of its King. In this doctrine the Biblical view of the unique significance of the connection between this people and this land reaches its climax.

PART TWO

INTERPRETATION AND
TRANSFIGURATION

INTERPRETATION AND TRANSFIGURATION

THE GIFT OF RAIN

O N EXAMINING the testimony of the Bible we have seen how God's association with the unity of Israel and Canaan is represented, in natural terms, by the gift of rain. This brings home to the peasantry more directly than anything else how dependent it is on the mercy of Heaven. The people as such prays for help and liberation in extraordinary situations in disaster and danger, under the impact of great historical shocks; but alongside these occasional crises, the troubles of life on this Palestinian soil, the faithful acceptance of the life it offers, suffering from drought and trust in the giver of rain recur, if not with absolute regularity yet again and again in the natural course of things. In post-Biblical times, as long as a nucleus of the people lives in the land, this basic feeling takes on a more elaborate and significant form.

The Talmudic treatise ' Taanit ', that is to say, Fasting, is devoted fundamentally to fasting and praying for the coming of the expected rain, especially when it fails to come for an unusually long time. It is a particularly beautiful example of the intimate connection between Halakha and Haggada, between those passages which discuss the ' course ', the right course of life, the right fulfilment of the demands of life, and those which, whether they link up directly or only indirectly with the former, bring in life itself, in stories, descriptions and discussions referring back again and again to the testimony of the Bible : the Halakha tries to preserve the essence of Sinai but the Haggada that of Canaan, and both work together, for not only does Canaan need the word of Sinai but Sinai also needs the reality of Canaan, in which the word is to be realized. When one of the later Babylonian masters of the Talmud, one of the great teachers of Sura and Pumbedita, speaks of the nature of Canaan and of life lived in this nature, then memory and hope speak merged into one, the Biblical past and the Messianic future stand on the horizon together.

The rain beats down through this treatise on fasting, not the ordinary familiar rain, but the long-yearned-for rain that is now at last descending whose sound testifies that it is the rain of God. At the same time it is not rain that might fall anywhere, but definitely and incomparably Palestinian rain, autumn rain and spring rain, which, like no other rain, is regarded not as the end of an assured sequence of climatic events but as the eternal renewal of God's mercy. Not only what has come down to us here of what was said in the land itself but also of what was said in Babylon, is concerned with *Palestinian* rain.

The Mishna, on which this treatise, like all those which it sets out to explain and supplement, is based, begins by enquiring from what time of the year the sentence called the ' rain-might ' is to be introduced into daily prayers. It is called the ' rain-might ' because in the months in which it is to be said it is incorporated into a blessing of which the first words are : ' Thou art mighty '. In its original version the prayer runs as follows : ' Thou art mighty, none is so strong as Thee, there is none beside Thee who makest the wind blow and the rain fall, who sustainest life, revivest the dead and art great in helping '. All at once we find ourselves in a world of faith in which rainfall and resurrection belong together. How is this to be understood? One of the teachers gives as a reason for the introduction of the words ' who makest the wind blow and the rain fall ' into the blessing of which the subject is man's life and death the fact that rain is just as important as the resurrection; another disputes this, not because he attaches greater importance to the resurrection but vice versa. This discussion does not bring us any nearer understanding the problem. To make it easier reference is usually made to the 146th Psalm and other passages in the Bible where the manifold activities of God's goodness are enumerated ; none of the passages can be compared with this blessing, however, in which the natural and the supernatural stand alongside each other so directly and abruptly. This is precisely what underlies the strange combination : the simple certainty that from God's point of view the distinction between ' natural ' and ' supernatural ' which has become so familiar to us, does not exist, that for Him—and the prayer is in fact addressed to Him quite concretely—the rain is no more natural than the resurrection and the resurrection no more miraculous than the rain. For Him

the two spheres are not distinct; He sends the rain that the earth
may ever be fruitful and He sends his 'dew of the powers of
light' on the 'land of ghosts' so that the dead may rise (Isaiah
26, 19). The Gemara gives forcible expression to this insight in
our treatise when it says : 'Three keys are in the hand of the Holy
One, blessed be He, that have not been delivered into the hands
of an emissary. And they are the key of rain, the key of birth and
the key of the revival of the dead.' The opening of the clouds is
here presented as of no less importance than the opening of the
womb and the latter as of no less importance than the opening
of the grave : all three are personal activities which God reserves
for Himself. Thus one can go so far as to risk making the almost
even more audacious statement that a day of rain is like the day
on which heaven and earth were created : the preservation of the
world is not subsidiary to its creation and not merely the running
down of a clockwork wound up once and for all time but an ever
renewed divine action. In what follows, however, the statement
about the 'key of the rain' is modified in a curious way. 'The
land of Israel,' we read here, 'was created first and the whole
world afterwards.' This priority in the beginning of time is
followed by a corresponding priority throughout all time : 'The
Holy One, blessed be He, waters the land of Israel Himself,
but he sends an emissary to water the whole world'. The Biblical
distinction between Egypt, that is provided for by its river, and
Canaan for which God Himself cares unceasingly, is widened into
a distinction between the land of Israel and the whole of the rest
of the world : only Israel receives the life-giving outpouring
directly from the hand of God. And a cognate Midrash says :
'He has given all lands servants to serve them. Egypt drinks from
the Nile, Babylon from the rivers, but things are ordered otherwise in the land of Israel; there the men sleep in their beds and
God sends down the rain to them'. Palestine is the land of God's
immediate care, for it is—this point will be developed later—the
centre of His world-plan and the goal of its fruitfulness is the
salvation of the whole world. This is the reason why there are
great teachers who rank any day of rain higher than the day on
which the Tora was given from Mount Sinai. It is true that the
reason given for this evaluation in one Midrash is that the Revelation gives joy only to Israel whereas rain gives joy to all
creatures, but there is no doubt that that is not the original idea,

—here too the argument hinges on Palestine. The word went forth from Sinai but the land of Israel is to prepare the realization of the word.

Why, on the other hand, is rain often withheld from this land for a time? Precisely on account of those who obstruct the realization of the Word by causing mischief among the people or otherwise hindering its development into the people of God : the robbers, the slanderers, the insolent, those who support almsgiving in public but do not contribute themselves, those who do not want to study the Tora. And yet why does the rain come all the same? Because of those who have remained faithful. When they, the faithful ' lay their souls in their hands ' and pray, the long-withheld rain comes down. Some of them live in great need and do not pray for their lot to be improved, in fact they do not even accept what is sent to them by a miracle; but when the land is threatened with drought, they pray for rain and it comes. Among those who pray are great teachers of the law such as Rabbi Akiba; he walks up to the sacred ark and says, apparently connecting the terms for God ' our Father' and ' our King', the one rooted in nature, the other in history,[1] for the first time and thereby establishing their connection in the liturgy (a connection which expresses the fundamentals of what the Semite has to say to his god as an individual and as a people): ' Our Father, our King, we have no other King but Thee alone! Our Father, our King, have mercy on us for Thy sake', and the rain comes—which, as others have prayed in vain, is attributed to Akiba's forbearing attitude to his fellow-men. But among those who pray there are also great sinners like the man who hires out prostitutes and dances and beats the drum at their feasts, but in the midst of all this sells his bed to save from prostitution a woman whom he sees weeping because her husband is in prison and who can think of no other way of setting him free than by becoming a prostitute; in a time of drought a rabbi sees in a dream that that same man must pray for rain to come—he too is numbered among the faithful.

Akiba's saying implies that it is not a question of merit being rewarded; everything depends rather on the grace of the Father and the King alone. But the story of the ' Fivefold sinner ' supple-

[1] Buechler, *Types of Jewish-Palestinian Piety*, p. 220, assumes without reason that the two terms had already become synonymous at that time.

ments this confession of faith in a remarkable way: the grace of God tries as it were to find some human merit to which it can relate itself, not necessarily a display of lifelong virtue but sometimes the spontaneous sacrificial action of someone otherwise very much bound up with the lower things of this world, some action by which the doer himself is more surprised than anyone else, one of those actions in which the sublime nature of man created in the image of God triumphs more than in all ordinary virtue. Such an example brings home quite concretely the mystery of the change of heart, the mystery to which the divine grace makes response. This is the kind of thing that this God expects from His people in order to give them His rain and His grace. Here we penetrate more deeply into the religious substance that Israel owes to the dependence of its land and its peasantry on the weather.

The stories of Honi, the 'drawer of circles', which have their setting in an earlier age, about two centuries before the prayer of Akiba, take us a step further. Honi is a 'Hasid', a man, that is to say, devoted to God, whose heart is open to his fellow-men and with a reputation for 'clean hands'. Besought, in a time of drought, to pray for rain he climbs the mount of the Temple and prays, but in vain. Then he draws a circle or digs a round pit (which of the two is not certain), puts himself inside it and declares to the Lord of the world that His, God's children, have turned to Him because he has stood before God 'as a member of the household', an intimate, confidential servant to whom the master listens, and now he swears by the great name of God that he will not move from the spot until God takes pity on His children and sends them rain. Then the rain falls, at first only in drops, finally in full measure. But afterwards, when the sun appears again and the people come out into the fields to gather mushrooms, Rabbi Simon ben Shetah, the man who 'restored the earlier authority of the Tora', sends word to Honi that he would excommunicate him if he were not Honi. But he cannot proceed against him as his behaviour towards God is like that of a spoilt child constantly importuning its father with wishes all of which are granted to it. This is a strange story and the heart of it seems to be concerned with magic and conjuration. It can only be understood if one bears two things in mind. First, the importance attached to the filial relationship to God both in Honi's address to God and in Rabbi Simon's message to Honi. There is an atmosphere of nearness to God, of intimate intercourse with Him in the story, in which magic cannot thrive. The second point to note is the description of Honi which we find in Josephus: he calls him an upright man 'beloved by God'; this description must be read in connection with the words that another man of prayer, Nicodemus ben Gorion, uses in a story in the same Talmudic treatise, in order to beg for rain: 'Lord of the world, make it known that Thou hast beloved men in thy world! 'But to understand both properly one must also bear in mind those words of the Bible (Deuteronomy 7, 7 f.; 9, 4 ff.) in which Israel is warned not to imagine that God had led it out of Egypt and brought it to Canaan because of its superior numbers or merit: He did it only because he loved Israel. Even the most noble action acquires no claim to the favour of God; he is glad to look upon it in His mercy but He is not moved by the deserts of His children but only by His own love. The 'beloved ones' like Honi are the living symbol of Israel itself and the ever renewed gift of rain the living symbol of the divine gift of the land to the people.

The Jerusalem version of our treatise summarizes the divine reasons for the gift of rain in the following words: 'The rain falls for the sake of three things: for the sake of the land, for the sake of the Hesed and for the sake of sufferings'. Hasidism is the way of life and thought of the 'Hasidim' of whom Honi is one; the main emphasis here is on love towards one's fellow-men, but even the learning of the Tora can take place with or without Hesed, on a basis of pure love or without it (Sukka 49b.) The term 'sufferings' makes one think first of all of the fasting that was ordered as a form of prayer for rain and which gave the treatise its name; but the meaning is much more comprehensive. The following saying has come down to us from Rabbi Simon ben Yohai, the mysterious master of early Talmudic doctrine: 'The Holy One, may He be blessed, has given three things to Israel and all of them He has given only through suffering: the Tora, the land of Israel and the world to come'. Here too, therefore, what applies to the rain also applies to the land itself. In both sayings we see the operation of the great teaching on the meaning of suffering which was given its decisive shape in the age of the Babylonian exile as we find it in the prophecies of 'Deutero-

Isaiah' on the suffering 'servant of the Lord'. There is an acceptance of suffering for the sake of God, for the sake of preparing the way for His Kingdom. To this doctrine, which was further developed in the Talmudic concept of the ' chastisements of love', there is now added its late counterpart: it is God's will that His great gifts should be acquired again and again through the acceptance of suffering. This is symbolized by the fasting for rain just as the gift of the land is symbolized by the gift of rain. One thing, however, is to be particularly noted in the sayings on the three things for whose sake (literally : ' for whose merit ') the rain falls : that the land comes first. The rain falls above all to please the land, and only in the second place to please the 'Hasidim' and those who willingly accept suffering.

But in what sense is the personal care which God bestows on the land of Israel to be understood? Must it be assumed that He neglects the other lands? The Midrash sets another sentence from the Bible against the words ' a land which the Lord thy God visits '. In God's answer to Job out of the whirlwind He reminds him (32, 26) that it is He, God, who causes it to rain on the wilderness where no man is—even there His care does not cease. It is true that it is also said of him (Psalms 121, 4): ' Behold He that keepeth Israel shall neither slumber nor sleep ', but that it is not merely Israel that he keeps is stated in another verse (Job 12, 10): ' In whose hand is the soul of every living thing'; of the newly built sanctuary in Jerusalem God says to Solomon (1 Kings 9, 3), 'Mine eyes and mine heart shall be there perpetually ', but it is also said (Zechariah 4, 10): ' the eyes of the Lord run to and fro through the whole earth ' and in the Book of Proverbs (15, 3): ' The eyes of the Lord are in every place, beholding the evil and the good.' In all this there is no contrast: God promises the sanctuary that His eyes will be as it were only there, but just because they are there they are in all places; and the other statement means that God only keeps Israel, but by keeping Israel He keeps everything, which means that Israel is the medium through which God preserves and keeps humanity as a whole. And likewise the land of Israel is the medium through which God transmits His care for the whole earth. This idea, which is a continuation of the national universalism of the prophets, also manifests the parallelism of people and land.

Haggadic thought is not a logical system. The Talmud is

essentially the deposit of innumerable discussions and the Haggada is no exception. But certain basic concepts and principles clearly emerge from the conflict of opinions, and just as there is a valid Halakha in spite of all the Halakhian controversies, so there is also an authoritative Haggada. The situation here is the same. Beyond all the differences of views on the subject, the special mercy shown to this land is held as a direct certainty.

To characterize this special grace of God, the later masters of the Talmud tell fabulous stories of the fertility of the land, particularly as it once was. The wine from a single vine fills six hundred casks every year, a single peach is enough to feed four men, and a fox builds its lair in the upper part of a turnip. These are not idle tales; the writers cannot find images enough to describe the favour by which this land has been continually blessed.

It is not a blessing, however, that falls into the laps of the idle. God's gracious favour is destined for the work of the man on the field which he has been set to till, for Israel's work in its own land. The Haggada regards planting as an imitation of God. 'From the beginning of His creation of the world', the Midrash relates, 'the Holy, blessed be He, has chiefly concerned Himself with planting, as it is said: "And God the Lord planted a garden in Eden". So too you, when you come into the land, are to concern yourselves chiefly with planting.' No other occupation is more important, nothing must be allowed to distract from it. 'If your hand is busy with planting and they say to you: "Messiah is come!", finish your planting first and then go out and receive Him.'

This land is not merely the land of special favour, it is also the land of special work. To the sentence in the Bible which tells how God fetches Abraham from his home and father's house and bids him go into the land 'that I shall show thee', the Midrash adds a story that shows great understanding of Abraham's situation. Abraham has received the command from a divine voice not to travel into a definite land but to move on until he comes into a land where the voice will tell him that this is where he must stay. From this point the Midrash goes on: 'While Abraham was travelling through Aram-Naharaim and the Aram of Nahor he saw the people eating and drinking and acting wantonly. Then he

said : ' Let me have no share in this land ! ' But when he reached
the slopes of Tyre and saw the people busy with weeding at
weeding-time and hoeing at hoeing-time he said : ' Let me have
a share in this land ! ' Then the Holy One, may He be blessed,
said to him : " I will give this land to thy seed." ' The land whose
people carefully tends the soil entrusted to it and carries out the
seasonal tasks of the land at their proper time, is the land of
true grace.

ASSOCIATION AND SEPARATION

BOTH the people and the land of Israel are elected by God. But
—and the Haggada sees this quite clearly—there is naturally a
fundamental difference between the two elections. The people is
chosen in a definite moment of history : it does not yet exist as a
people but a man is chosen from one of the families to become the
tribal father from whose sons, grandsons and great-grandsons
one is chosen to form the original stock of the people. The people
arises in the course of history, in fact, and thus its election takes
place in the succession of the generations, in a series of acts of
elimination and selection. But the land, on the other hand, is as
such not the product of history but a part of Creation; therefore
its election must have taken place in the very act of the Creation
itself. It is true that it is said of Israel that God created the nations
and chose one of them in particular; but until the human substance, which can be the concrete subject of election, actually
exists this can obviously only be an event in the mind of God.
It is not thus with the land : its actual election is part of the
original act of Creation. The two elections are also represented
in the image of the heave-offering : God heaves as it were a
heave-offering from the lands and from the peoples. But this
image does not in any way alter the unavoidable difference : the
election of the land not only has precedence in time, it belongs
to a different sphere of time; it is not an event of history but of
Creation. But the difference goes even deeper than that. What is
elected in history can be young and thus Israel is a young people
which arose long after the human race had been divided into
peoples. It is not thus with what has been elected in Creation.
to be elected in the Creation means to be created as something
elect; the act of Creation and that of Election coincide. Like the

Tora and the sanctuary, the land of Israel is also part of the original Creation. The words in the Proverbs of Solomon, 'the earliest dust layer of the world,' are applied to it. The term *tebel* is used here for 'world'. Some go further and say that the land of Israel is the real *tebel*, it is called *tebel* because it is flavoured, *metubal*, with everything—every other land has some things and lacks others, but 'there is no lack of anything' in Israel, it has everything. This land is a microcosm, a model of the whole world.

Election is Love. Just as Moses tells the people (Deuteronomy 7, 7 f.) that God did not choose them for any reason except that He loved them so the Midrash makes God say: ' I love this land more than anything else'. And because He loves both the land and the people, He decides to bring them together. 'I will,' He says, ' cause Israel that I love to move into the land that I love.' Thus a king marries a manservant and a maidservant whom he wishes well. In this action there is, however, far more than the will of a king. God has decided that those who belong to each other shall be joined, for He created and chose them as belonging to each other, as suiting each other and being dependent on each other. And He did all this, both creation and election and the marrying of the elected, because of his purpose for the Creation and for the perfecting of His creation: the union of people and land is intended to contribute to the perfecting of the world in order to become the Kingdom of God.

For the Haggadic interpretation of the Bible as for the Bible itself everything depends on Israel's appropriation of the land being understood both by the generations of the people itself and by the nations of the world as what it is: as an event intended and carried out by God for His own ends. God's leading of Israel into Canaan is of central importance among the many instances of God's leading a people into the land where it is to settle. This is already made manifest in the fact that the revelation that of all the nations only Israel knows, while it is being led, that it is the Creator of the world, its Lord and Redeemer, that is leading it, occurs at the beginning of the Exodus from Egypt. Israel enters the land because it is being led by Him and is serving His will. This fact is rightly stressed both by the Bible and the Haggada, for without it neither Israel nor its history can be understood. The famous question, why the Tora does not begin with the instructions for the Feast of the Passover, for this is after all the first commandment and the Tora is there to command and not to narrate, and the further question why was the history of Creation made known to Israel, must be read in this context. The words of the Psalms (111, 6) are quoted in reply: 'He hath told his people the power of His works, giving them the property of nations.' For if the peoples come and reproach Israel, saying, 'You are a people of robbers, you who have conquered the lands of seven nations', Israel can point out to them that its God created heaven and earth, that the whole earth is His and that He can apportion land to whom He wills—'according to His will He gave you the land and according to His will He has taken it away from you and given it to us'. This does not mean at all that all invasions of other lands are to be considered equally justified because they are willed by God or even that all acts of violence of one people against another are justifiable. The essential point is that Israel heard the will of the Lord of the world at the beginning of its expedition to Canaan and conquered the land in the perfect and well-founded faith that it was accomplishing His will. With however little or much right in each case the nations can accuse each other of being robbers, their charge against Israel is totally unjust for it acted under authority and in the confident knowledge of its authorization. The revelation, the faith in it and the action following from this faith, are what differentiate Israel from the other peoples not merely 'religiously' but also historically. At all times there have been peoples who have given divine labels to their passions and interpreted the acts of violence born of their own greed for possessions, power and destruction as commanded by these divinities; at all times there have been peoples whose actions and self-appraisement were more honest and pure; but so far as we are able to judge from the records, no other people has ever heard and accepted the command from heaven as did the people of Israel. So long as it sincerely carried out the command it was in the right and is in the right in so far as it still carries it out. Its unique relationship to its land must be seen in this light. Only in the realm of perfect faith is it the land of this people. But perfect faith does not mean faith in oneself, in one's own rights or one's own *Lebensraum* or anything of that kind, but faith in the commander and the command, in the giver of the commission and in his commission. Where a command and a faith are present,—in certain historical situations conquest need not be robbery; but conquest is not by any means a historical necessity, for God is the Lord of history, not history the lord of God.

Another passage in the Midrash shows how profoundly the question as to the justice of the appropriation of the land has occupied the people's mind. 'There are three places in respect of which the nations of the world cannot torment Israel and say, "they were stolen by you", and these are: the Cave of Makhpela, Joseph's tomb and the Temple.' Like so many statements in the Haggada this one also has a vast background. At first sight it seems that no more is implied in the statement than that the two burial-places, the one in Hebron and the other in Shechem (Genesis 33, 9; 50, 5; Joshua 24, 32),·and the threshing-floor of the Jebusite on which the sanctuary was built were acquired by an agreement between the buyer and the seller. But the Midrash obviously wishes to hint at the significance of the fact that it was burial ground and sacred ground of which the purchase is reported in the Bible: first, the graves of the fathers who, lying in their caverns, as it were kept the ground occupied and defended the original claim of the elect to this land in the stillness of death, until the people came and realized the claim, and who continued to defend it in the midst of a foreign people after the exile and renewed exile of the people; then the sanctuary in Jerusalem, destined by God from the beginning of creation as the place which He intended His name to 'inhabit', and thus a token and a pledge, even after its destruction, of the eternal meeting of heaven and earth in this land.

The significance of the ancestral tomb for the people's claim to the land emerges even more clearly from the stories of the dividing of the inheritance between Jacob and Esau. After the death of his father, Jacob exchanges everything he has brought with him from without for gold and gives Esau the choice of taking this or his share in the cave of Makhpela. Esau says: 'What is the use of this cave to me?' or 'A grave can be found anywhere!'; he chooses the gold and leaves the land with his family. The burial-place in which only the elect, only Abraham and not Lot, Isaac and not Ishmael rest, remains the possession of Jacob and hence the land too, for the cave is also a token and pledge of the promise of the land; for the father of the people that is to inherit the land it is more important to possess the cave than all the property in the world.

But for all that the Haggada does not forget that the Promise was given to Abraham so that he, that is, the people deriving from him, 'may become a blessing' and on this condition. 'Three things', the Midrash says, 'have been given subject to a condition: the land of Israel, the Temple, and the kingship of the house of David.' The Bible is quoted to verify this statement. They are the three things which have been taken from faithless Israel but which continue to exist and are to be given back to an Israel that has returned to its faith; the land of Israel continues in its forsakenness, the Temple only survives in its heavenly prototype, and the house of David is unknown and forgotten. All three will return in a new glory: the historical sphere as represented by the land, the religious, of which the sanctuary is the centre, and the Messianic in which both spheres will become one.

The Haggada is deeply penetrated by the consciousness, derived from the Bible, that this decay of the supreme possessions of the people is due to the falling away of the people from the Giver. Here too the land is in the foreground. The Biblical teaching on the polluting and disintegrating influence of the misdeeds of the people on the soil of the land is taken up and elaborated by the Haggada. Three kinds of wickedness are attributed to this influence; the first is bloodshed, the second idolatry, but the third is pride. 'Whoever is proud causes the pollution of the land and the withdrawal of the Shekhina (the world-inhabiting hypostasis of God)', the Shekhina which the humble cause to dwell among men on earth. It is significant that just as evil an effect is attributed to pride as to bloodshed and idolatry. This too must certainly be understood in connection with the Election. Whoever believes in the Election and fulfils its commission in all humility gives sustaining power to the land and helps to keep the Shekhina near to it; but whoever makes the Election a motive for haughtiness, whoever imagines himself protected and exalted by it, instead of being laid under an obligation and set to work by it, weakens the land and sets the Shekhina against it. People and land are connected by the Election but they can only remain connected if and so long as the commission which it implies is carried out by the people in humble work for God.

And God himself suffers when the punishment has been carried

out and the people and the land have been separated from one
another. He leaves the people in the melting furnace of exile and
yet he cries : ' Would that my sons were in the land of Israel, even
though they pollute it !' Words such as these display the alogical,
supralogical character of the Haggada : it is not concerned with
an abstractly correct theology, it is not afraid to make God Himself
contradict Himself, if only such contradiction can give direct
expression to the fact that punishment and grace dwell closely
together in God's relationship to an Israel in exile from its
land.

God's faithfulness to the forsaken land is painted in ever new
pictures which betray not the slightest fear of anthropomorphism.
It is said that the Shekhina has departed from it ? On the contrary, she does not even depart from the shattered sanctuary.
' The Shekhina,' we read, ' will not move from the West wall
in eternity ', that is, from the last remains of the Temple. To this
are applied the words in the Song of Solomon, where the bride
says of her beloved : ' He stands there behind our wall '. This
is God, the Faithful One, standing behind the west wall of His
shattered sanctuary. Another picture (that must be understood in
this context) : God cries that He does not want to move into the
higher, the heavenly Jerusalem before He can move into the
lower, earthly Jerusalem, or—according to a later, Cabbalistic
version—before Israel can move into the earthly Jerusalem again.
But there is an even more daring picture. When the men of Israel,
so we are told, refused to sing before the idols of Babel the songs
that had been sung in the Temple in Jerusalem and joyfully
allowed themselves to be slain because of their refusal, God
swore : ' If I forget thee, Jerusalem, let my right hand forget its
function !'

The land of Israel is sick but it shall recover. ' From the day on
which the Temple was destroyed the land has suffered from the
evil that have befallen its inhabitants. Like a man who is ill and
no longer has the strength to stand on his feet, the land has not
the strength to bring forth its fruits. But in the future the Holy
One, blessed be He, will send down the dew of revival and will
give new life to the dead.'

In the Land and Outside it

IN ORDER to grasp the inferences that were drawn from the fact of the fundamental relationship between the people and the land, concerning the difference between this land and the rest of the world, three sentences in the Haggada must be borne in mind.

The first is contained in the well-known story, recurring in two different variants, of the teachers of the law who go abroad to receive instruction or for some other certainly no less sacred reason, but who, as soon as they arrive at the frontier, are so overwhelmed by the thought of the land that, weeping, they tear their clothes in pieces and return home with the cry, 'Dwelling in the land of Israel outweighs all the commandments of the Tora', referring to quotations from the Bible (Deuteronomy 11, 31 f., cf. 12, 28 f.) in which the fulfilment of the commandments and settlement in the land are linked together. This reference to the Bible explains the ultimate meaning of their cry : the true and perfect fulfilment of the commandments is possible only in the whole life of the people that settles in the land of Israel, therefore the settlement is the precondition of the true and perfect fulfilment of the commandments and thus it alone outweighs all the commandments, in so far as it is intended to fulfil them without it. This is the only way to explain that an importance is attributed to dwelling in the land that exceeds all the other commandments : for it alone makes the true and perfect fulfilment of the others possible.

The much discussed and much interpreted saying, 'Everyone that lives in the land of Israel is like the man that has a god and everyone that lives abroad is like the man that has no god', goes still further. One is inclined to see in the sentence merely the paradoxically intensified expression of the value that is attached to dwelling in the land. But such an expression too must be grounded in a genuine basic intuition. The saying is founded on two quotations from the Bible. The first is the divine declaration contained in the law on the year of Jubilee (Leviticus 25, 38) that God had led Israel out of Egypt, 'to give you the land of Canaan and to be your God'; the verse is obviously taken as meaning that the giving of the land is the precondition of being the God of the

people. The other is David's complaint before Saul about the men
(Samuel 26, 19) who ' have driven me out this day from abiding
in the inheritance of YHVH, as if to say (not, ' saying ' as it is
usually translated) : Go, serve other gods.' This verse is obviously
taken as meaning that a man who is driven out of the community of his people and his land may be treated as if he were
no longer able to serve his God outside this community. If we
take the two verses together, according to this interpretation the
meaning of the original saying proves to be : the Israelite who
lives outside his land ' has ' of course a god no less than he who
dwells in the land, but he ' is like ' one who has no god since,
precisely because he is an Israelite, he can only attain a proper
fellowship with God, only serve Him aright, as a participant in the
common life of people and land : because God has promised
Israel that He will be its God, *as a people* and because He has
given it *the land* as the precondition thereof.

The third of the sentences from the Haggada is also to be
understood from this point of view. God says to Jacob, when He
commands him to return to the homeland (Genesis 31, 3):
' Return unto the land of thy fathers and to thy kindred, and I
will be with thee—thy father is waiting for thee, thy mother wait-
eth for thee, I myself am waiting for thee.' It is true that He had
once promised, in the dream of the ladder reaching to heaven
(28, 15) that he would be with him and keep him ' in all places
whither thou goest ', and Jacob knew and confessed (31, 5) that
He had been with him away from the homeland,—and yet : God
waits for him in the homeland, for only there is perfect communion with Him possible, only there can Jacob *as the
progenitor of the people* hold fellowship with the God of Israel.
What the Midrash makes God say to Jacob it makes Him say to
Israel : ' I myself am waiting for him.'

To see how seriously, how realistically such words were taken
if not by everyone, at least by some, one must study the reports
on the lives of some persons affected by them. We find the most
beautiful example in what is told us of the life of a well-known
teacher of law of the fourth century, the Rabbi Zeïra. We learn
that when he wanted to go from Babylon to Palestine he shunned
his teacher because the latter said that anyone who did that was
violating a commandment, since it was written (Jeremiah 27, 22):
' They shall be carried to Babylon and there shall they be.' He

knew that this was not so but he did not want to contradict his
teacher, perhaps the subject did not seem to him to be one for
discussion at all but of purely practical decision : he did not
want to say anything at all, but simply to go there. The journey
meant something quite different to him than a removal from one
land to another : it seemed to him as if he were moving from
one world to another. Therefore he spent a hundred days fasting
to 'forget' the teaching methods of the Babylonian School with
its pointed dialectic and so as not to be disturbed by memories
of it in the land of Israel. It needed an enormous effort to rid his
mind of a method which he had come to take as a matter of
course, so familiar to him had it become ; but this effort had to
be made in order truly to assimilate the teaching of the homeland and make it his own. The break is so complete that in
Palestine he calls his Babylonian colleagues ' foolish '.

When he reaches the Jordan, Zeïra does not find a ferry but
he cannot wait so he pulls himself over by the ferry rope. A
heretic who sees this mocks at him : ' You overhasty people that
[once on Mount Sinai, saying ' We will act and we will hear ']
sent on your mouths in advance of your ears—you still persist
in being in too great a hurry !' But Zeïra replies : ' The place
which was not granted to Moses and Aaron, who is to say that
it will be granted to me !' He has no assurance that he will
enter the land ; perhaps, in the short time he is waiting for the
ferry something may happen that will prevent him, therefore,
now that he is on his way, he must not lose even a moment. But
there is something still deeper behind his words : the knowledge
that God waits for every single member of Israel; just as the
people once declared itself ready for action at the first call of
God, before it even knew what was demanded of it, so each
individual's duty is unhesitatingly to follow God's call into the
land.

Zeïra, who was conspicuous in appearance, small and dark-
skinned, must have looked just like the Babylonian that he was.
Only if that was so can the trick be understood which a butcher
played on him soon after his arrival. He declares that a pound of
meat costs fifty pieces of money and a slap in the face. After
some discussion Zeïra agrees, since he assumes that this must be
the local custom. There is a counterpart to this in the story of
another butcher who, besought by Zeïra to weigh the meat well,

lets fly at him: 'Get out of here, you Babylonian, whose forefathers destroyed the Sanctuary!' Zeïra's first reaction to the
insult is to wonder: 'Aren't my forefathers the same as his?'
But when he then goes into the house of instruction and hears
the words of the Song of Solomon 'If she is a wall' being expounded thus: 'If Israel had come out of exile like a wall, the
Sanctuary would not have been destroyed for a second time', he
says: 'That ignorant man has taught me well.' The spiritual
impulse which brought him here from Babylon finds its strongest
expression in this simple statement. He feels himself as a participant in the guilt of all the generations who had not returned to
the homeland in the six centuries during which the second Temple
was still standing: yes, indeed, it was they who destroyed the
Temple, and he, one of their descendants, who has come as a
single person into the land of the ruined Temple, must take the
accusation on his head.

There is something else, however, that such anecdotes reveal:
how seriously he takes the utterances of those who reside in the
land. Even when the speakers are ignoramuses, a knowledge un-
conscious and inaccessible to them speaks out of their mouth.
Zeïra says: 'Even the mere conversation of the Palestinians is
instructive.' The spirit has in fact held sway in this land from
time immemorial. And it operates not only in the human beings
but also in the earth and in the air. Rabbi Zeïra says: 'The air
of the land of Israel makes [its inhabitants] wise'.

And finally his peculiar conception of the dawn of the
Messianic age is also a fruit of this special relationship to the
land. He hears his companions discussing when the Redemption
will come and what must happen for it to come, but he says:
'I pray you, do not put it off', and supports his argument with
some drastic comparisons: just as one finds something unexpectedly, just as a scorpion bites unexpectedly, so Messiah will
come when no one is thinking of him. This too is, as we have
said, a fruit of Zeïra's basic attitude to dwelling in the land:
living in the land and in the midst of the people, doing the will of
God *as a people*, only this, not discussing the Redemption, not
pondering over it, not making frantic exertions to bring it about,
only living in the land as God's people will bring Messiah 'when
no one is thinking of him.'

All this must be seen and heard as a whole in order to understand thoroughly the expository and illuminating teaching of the Talmudic-Midrashic age on the meaning of dwelling in the land of Israel: the three sayings—the one concerning the settlement which outweighs all the commandments, the second concerning the settler who, in contrast to the man living abroad is like one who has a god, and the third which makes God say: 'I myself am waiting for thee'—and this exemplary man, the little Rabbi Zeïra, who lives in the land really, with the whole might of his soul and knows that the Redemption will come when no one is thinking about it.

PART THREE

THE VOICE OF THE EXILE

THE VOICE OF THE EXILE

THE HEART OF A POET

(*On the Book 'Kusari'*)

'APOLOGETICS' are usually taken as meaning that species of religious literature which aims at demonstrating the truth of doctrines of faith while refuting the arguments put forward by those who deny this truth. This definition is only partially applicable to Jewish apologetics. In accordance with the fundamental character of Judaism, which sets out to be not a system of articles of faith but of a life lived in faith, Jewish apologetics are concerned, it is true, with proving the truth of that which is believed but even more with proving the rightness of that which is lived. This is the point of view from which the inner sequence of its masterpiece, the 'Kusari' of Jehuda Halevi is to be understood. To which it should be added that the author of this work was a great poet and, however theoretical a book a poet may write, it will always contain two elements, though they may be somewhat hidden at times : the portrayal of human situations and the utterance of the poet's own soul.

Although the work steers clear of description and narration, the situation in which the dialogue of the book 'Kusari' takes place arises from a poetic vision. This King of the Khazars who, informed by a dream of the fundamental defects of his existence, starts conversations with wise men to learn how he is to overcome them, is, although his personality is only lightly touched on, no abstract concept but a human being. And it is of importance that the angel in the dream does not reveal to him that his faith is wrong or his convictions inadequate, but that he is not living and acting as it pleases the Creator. Thus at the very start we are confronted with the basic tendency of Judaism to be concerned with the attitude to and ordering of life, with its distinction between life in conformity with the will of God and life not in accordance therewith. Accordingly, in his conversations with the wise men, the King of the Khazars, despite the fact that he first

asks them ' about their faith ', is bent on learning how their ways
of life compare with his own.

Convictions based on pure thinking cannot be decisive in
themselves. Unmistakably hinting at the first Crusade the poet
puts an obvious reference to the fighting between Edom and
Ishmael, ' who have divided the inhabited world between them ',
into the mouth of the King : both the Christian and the Moslem
desire to serve God ; kill each other with this purpose in view and
are both certain that they will enter Paradise : both of them
cannot be right in any case, although one pious conviction is
pitted against another. The philosopher's answer that killing is
in itself contrary to reason, does not satisfy the King : in the
conceptual world of the philosophers it is certainly possible to
think but not to live, to think rightly but not to live rightly.
Prophets not philosophers show men the truth of *life* ; and some
who have not concerned themselves with lofty spiritual matters
have thus truth pointed out to them in ' true dreams ' (here the
Khazar King is obviously thinking of his own dream). There is
a mystery in the divine and in the souls of men that surpasses
the wisdom of the philosophers. The King does not question the
Christian and the Moslem sages to whom he now appeals, about
their faith alone, as he did the philosopher, but also about their
deeds. Both of them answer too dogmatically to convince the
questioner as to the bases of their religions : namely God's action
towards and in the world of man, actions that show man the
way for his own doing. If the philosopher only produced abstractions, it is true that the representatives of the two religions also
point to God's actual government of the world alongside general
remarks on His eternity and spirituality, but as expressed in
their dogmatic terminology, this government does not appear to
manifest itself in historical life and set the standard for personal
life; the Khazar King cannot find what he is looking for here.
Only now, and because both theologicans had referred to the
holy scriptures of Israel, does he also ask a Jew, although it had
been his original intention not to consult anyone belonging to this
outwardly and inwardly fallen race. It is a striking fact that he
now again asks only about faith, presumably because his experience has taught him that this is the only thing about which
he can obtain information. And in fact the Rabbi does answer
with a ' credo '. But this profession of faith is completely differ-

ON ZION 63

ent from the others. The Jew does not speak of the nature of
God but only of his activity in the history of Israel. It is history,
historical life in which he professes his faith; he speaks as if the
Jews had no faith apart from their history, but it is a history of
the deeds of God, it is history, experienced as something that takes
place between heaven and earth. The Jew regards the doctrines of
the other faiths as 'speculative': he does not believe that it is
possible to reach the point the King wants to reach on the paths
of theological dogma, that is to say, the point where one learns
of God's qualities in such a way as 'to become more like the
Creator in wisdom and justice'. The imitation of God cannot be
learnt from statements about His nature, but from the living
witness of His rule in human history and the whole essence of
the Jew attests what his words confess. The King is very soon
aware of that and the great conversation between the two of
them begins, the first part of which results in the Khazar's conversion to Judaism. It is true that this conversation embraces
heavenly as well as earthly things but always in relation to the
concrete, to the historical, to Israel. It is no accident that the
third, or middle section deals with the divine commandments laid
upon the life of the individual Jew and the Jewish people. Again
and again the Rabbi endeavours to show the King the vital relationship between God and Israel. In so doing he refrains from
an idealistic interpretation of his people, which would merely put
another purely intellectual conception in the place of historical
truth. The burden of the people's sufferings affects him deeply,
because for the majority of them it is an imposition, not something to be accepted freely. He knows well enough that only a
small part of the nation is brought by the pressure of the burden
to an attitude of humility towards God and His teaching. 'If, on
the other hand, we were to bear this exile and humiliation in
the proper way for the sake of God, then we should bring near
the liberation for which we are waiting.'

The difference between the promises of other religions to their
believers and those of the Tora is seen chiefly in the fact that,
in the former, bliss after death is promised to the obedient individual, whereas, in the latter to an Israel that fulfils the commandment the promise is made that 'Ye shall become my people'. And
this also includes—this is the first time the Rabbi mentions
Palestine—: 'Ye shall continue in the land that helps you to

reach this high level, for it is a holy land. Its fruitfulness or
sterility, its good or evil fortune depend, according to your deeds,
directly on the Divinity, while all the rest of the world depends
on the natural law.' Thus Jehuda Halevi takes up the Biblical-
Talmudic view of God's special care for Israel again by connecting it with the Biblical view of the influence of human actions
on the fate of the soil. The direct influence of human actions on
the history of the soil, as the Bible describes it in reference to
primitive times, he restricts, duing the historical period, to Palestine : only the soil of the land of Israel is now called to account
for the actions of the people, the rest of the inhabited earth is
subject solely to the laws of Nature and is secured by them. In this
way the mutual dependence of the people and the land of Israel
receives an emphasis all of its own.

In the first part of the book the Palestine motif is only sounded
for a moment and then vanishes, to be more fully developed in
the second part. The Rabbi who is now no longer merely giving
information but is teaching the proselyte, explains the nature
of the divine ' glory ', the Kavod. It is ' a beam of the divine
light which exerts its influence on His people in His land '. The
King of the Khazars acknowledges its effect on the people of
God. He has come to understand that the Divinity selects suitable
material for its purpose from the human race, in order to impart
itself directly to it ; but he finds it difficult to understand and
accept the view that any one part of the earth is to be described
as the land of God above all others. In answer the Rabbi points
to a mountain on which the best vines flourish : the noble vines
need this special soil which is more favourable to their growth
than any other, though they must be planted and cared for in the
right way in order to produce such grapes. The vines are the
Chosen People, 'the peculiar property and the Kernel', the
mountain is the land of Israel, the cultivation the actions which
must be performed in the land of Israel and cannot be performed
elsewhere ; but the fruit of the vineyard is the prophecy which is
Israel's exclusive possession. 'The peculiar property cannot
adhere to the divine in any other place, just as the vineyard can
only thrive on this mountain.' Prophecy has taken place only in
the land of Israel or in reference to it and for its sake. From
the earliest times the Revelation has come to pass within its
sphere. When he was found worthy Abraham was transferred

here from his own land, so that he might here attain his perfection; in the same way as a countryman finds the root of a good
fruit tree in the desert and transplants it to a soil favourable to its
development into a fruit tree. In Canaan the gift of prophecy
passes from Abraham to his seed. Jacob acknowledged the share
of the land in this gift when he attributed the vision that was
vouchsafed him not to the purity of his soul and not to the
strength of his faith but to the ' awe-inspiring' place. The gifts of
God seek out for themselves the natural terrain in which they
can fully develop; what God wants to impart to the world
through Revelation and what he has given to it in the Creation—
both aspire towards each other. Creation strives to approach
God but the Revelation strives to become embodied, it prepares
for itself within the realm of Nature the vessel most suited to
receive it, to give it life and bear it forth into the world. The
land of Israel was chosen to make the entire world upright; and
that is why it was intended for the tribes of Israel from the
' Generation of the Division of Tongues', from the time that the
primeval unity of mankind was broken up into nations and 'the
Most High gave possession to the nations'. The possession of
YHVH was kept for the people of YHVH. The days on which
this bond between the people and the land and their appointment
to a common task is celebrated, are called ' festive seasons of the
Lord', whilst the preparation for this task, which is spread over
the whole year, is called ' the service of YHVH'. Days of rest
are called ' Sabbaths of YHVH'. But the whole year during
which the soil takes a rest at the end of every seven years is
called a ' Sabbath of the land': so greatly has God bestowed his
special love on this land, so much does He desire to glorify Himself in it. But even the Sabbaths of YHVH and the festive seasons
of YHVH are dependent on the land, for one must base one's
calculations on it to ascertain the times at which the festivals
begin in every place in the inhabited world. Jehuda Halevi connects this with two sayings taken from the Haggadic tradition.
According to the first, Palestine is regarded as the ' centre of the
inhabited world' (the Haggada says, ' the centre of the world').
The other tells how Adam, after he had sinned, was taken from
the Garden of Eden to the land of Israel on the Sabbath eve to
till the soil there and how he began to count the days following
the six days of the Creation. From the beginning of time, Palestine

'the gate to heaven' has been the central and decisive factor in
space and time. Thus even today all people still revere this land,
although the Shekhina no longer allows itself to be seen here. All
religious communions make pilgrimage thither and seek after it,
'we alone fail to do so because of our exile and the oppression
which has been forced upon us'. This is a return of the sharp
self-criticism which we met in the distinction between the attitude
of the few and that of the many in Israel and which, for Jehuda
Halevi, is absolutely compatible with his high esteem of Israel:
he who is called to greatness is the most intensely threatened from
within.

The King requests the Rabbi to recite to him some of the wise
men's utterances on the high standing of Palestine. But instead of
quoting some of the many things that have been said in praise of
the land, its holiness and manifold blessings, he merely quotes
certain sayings about the importance of living in the land. It is
as though he positively intended to provoke the King to the
reproach with which he now replies to all the instructions—as if
he were drawing a final conclusion from them: 'If that is so,
then you are offending against the duty laid upon you by the
Tora, since you are not striving to reach this place, not making
it the place where you live and die, despite the fact that you
pray: "Have mercy on Zion for it is the home of our life" and
believe that the Shekhina will return there. . . . So all your
kneelings and prostrations in that direction are mere hypocrisy or
a thoughtless routine.' And the Rabbi accepts the reproach as
justified. 'You shame me, king of the Khazars', he says. This is in
entire accordance with the answer he gives to the King in the
first part of the conversation, when the King objects that the
humble bearing of the Jewish people is not voluntary but forced
on them: 'You have touched my weak spot, king of the
Khazars'. But although in the first case it is the people, in the
second the individual that is indicted—both are concerned with
the same issue: faith standing the test of daily life. Here we come
to the real kernel of the whole work, which had already appeared
at the beginning in the King's dream in which the angel told
him pointblank that his faith was pleasing to God but not his
life. At that time, he had not known, however, *how* to live.
Now he has discovered the secret by being instructed about
Israel's system of life. But he notices, first, how little the people

itself really puts this system into practice, truly that is to say, from the heart's intention, and that it only practices some of the highest virtues because external conditions make it impossible to transgress them; then he notices on the other hand, that even the man instructing him does not carry out in his own life everything he believes and proclaims. That is what Jehuda Halevi makes his King of the Khazars say to the Rabbi. That he draws it from the depths of his own heart is especially evident from the Rabbi's answer to the reproach. He says that what he is accused of, namely, omitting to return to the homeland, is precisely what 'frustrated the fulfilment of the divine promise for the second Temple': 'The Divinity was already prepared to come down again as before, if only they had all agreed with a joyful heart to return to the land. But only part of them returned; the majority and particularly the outstanding ones remained in Babylon and preferred to live as barely tolerated slaves as long as they were not separated from their homes and businesses. . . . Certainly, if we were ready to meet the God of our fathers with our whole hearts, we should obtain from him that which our fathers obtained in Egypt.' If, living as we do, we speak in our prayers of God 'leading back his Shekhina to Zion', it is of no more value than starlings' chatter. Here we feel that Jehuda Halevi has previously said to himself in the secret of his heart what he makes his Rabbi say to the King; we are listening to the utterance of the soul of a poet. A great soul and a great poetic gift are needed to express things in this way. The words grip us and are meant to grip us; for the purpose of the book is that these words shall not recede from our mind and memory until we reach its end where their full personal meaning will be revealed to us.

We hardly hear anything more of Palestine until nearly the end of the book; it is only mentioned in passing. It is as though all the essentials had already been dealt with and the unimportant things were to be passed over in silence. Indeed, it is as if there were a special purpose behind this silence; what is revealed to us right at the end is not to be prepared for by previous conversations about the land; what is to be revealed to us can be fully revealed to us only if it has not been prepared for in advance. The Rabbi's teaching comes to an end, therefore, directly after it has come nearest to dogmatic language and has thus departed

furthest from its real task. The conversation breaks off, and the
narrative style which had been entirely absent since from the
beginning of the second part, is resumed; we hear that the Rabbi
has now decided to leave the land of the Khazars to go up to
Jerusalem. How are we to understand this decision in relation to
the book? It is obvious that it has ripened since the King uttered
his rebuke. Did the rebuke itself have this effect? Or was it not
rather that he heard the reproach of his own heart speaking to
him in another's words? That, however, is not all. He had been
called to this King to tell him of the proper way to live. He had
told him the secret, he had told him of the corporeality of the
proper life, according to his knowledge of it as a son of Israel, that
is, of a corporeality based on the primeval relationship between a
chosen people and a chosen land; and what he said he had heard
as if he were saying it all to himself. Everything, so he had taught,
depends on living what one believes in; was he living what he
believed in? The King's reproach had cut him to the heart, but
in his answer he had beaten his own breast. Since then he had
deliberately kept silent on the subject: but in the silence the
resolve to do what he had hitherto left undone, had ripened.
And all this is again no mere contrivance or fabrication but part,
the concluding part of the poet's confession. He himself has made
the decision. But now the King who had reproved him for not
going to the land of Israel, tries to dissuade him: What could
he want there now that the Shekhina was no longer in the land?
After all, it was possible to participate in the nearness of God in
any place in the world by purity of intent. Why did he want to
expose himself to the dangers of that country? It is clear that, so
as not to lose the Rabbi, the King of the Khazars does not
hesitate to use arguments which have been contradicted by the
whole course of the conversation, and even by his own words:
he is now arguing that neither words nor actions are of decisive
importance, nowadays at least all places are of equal value as far
as religious matters are concerned and purity of intent is the one
thing needful. In his answer, however, the Rabbi uses his own
case to shed a practical light on the whole meaning of his teaching
on the concreteness of the religious life and on the need for
action. The misgivings which the King has expressed about the
journey now become intelligible within the context of the book
as a whole: they are intended to prepare the way for this answer

in which the confessions of the Rabbi and the author alike reach their peak. The Rabbi brings forward seven points—twice interrupted by objections from the Khazar, both of which lead, however, to important additions to this exposition.

Firstly: it is indeed true that the Shekhina is not to be found in the land of Israel today, because it only reveals itself in a definite place to a prophet or to a small company of people fulfilling the will of God and therefore well-pleasing in his sight; this direct perception of the Shekhina is promised us for the time 'when the Lord returns to Zion'. But the non-perceivable spiritual Shekhina dwells 'with every true-born Israelite whose deeds are honest, whose heart is pure and whose intention is wholly devoted to the God of Israel'. On the face of it this is no counter-argument, indeed it almost sounds like a substantiation of the Khazar's view, but a more careful listener will hear, between the lines, what Jehuda Halevi probably deliberately refused to say explicitly but which alone makes it possible to understand why he wrote what he did write. As the Shekhina which is attached to the true community of Israel has dwelt in each of the scattered parts of the people since the dispersion of the Assembly of Israel, that is, with every genuine, truly God-serving Jew, everyone of those who ascend to the Holy Land takes this presence with him and those who do this do not merely gather together the Assembly of Israel, but also lead to the re-concentration of the Shekhina itself in this place. To illuminate the ultimate significance of this is left to the end of the Rabbi's speech.

Secondly: as the land of Israel is of all lands the one hallowed to God, religious actions can only reach perfection there and certain commandments can only be fulfilled there. This means that the Jew can only serve God with the whole of his active life in Palestine; what is done in the lands of the Exile is necessarily imperfect since perfect action can only flourish in the land of Israel. The presupposition from which this second principle, and the one following proceed is that the holiness of the land has not been diminished by all the changes and chances of history.

Thirdly: not only do actions attain perfection in the land of Israel but the heart itself can only maintain its purity there. In order fully to understand this principle one must bear in mind the distinction between intent and action that runs right through

the book. The starting-point was that intent alone is not enough,
an upright active life must be added to it; this can, as we have
heard, only reach perfection in the Holy Land; but however pure
it is, intent itself is lacking a final, as it were natural and objective purity of spiritual substance, a purity which can enter the
soul only under the influence of the holiness of the land. Just as
the land perfects the active life, so too it perfects the soul.

Fourthly (once again the principle links up with the preceding
one): not merely the state of life and the soul, but also the all-
important relationship between God and man changes when the
latter ascends to the land of Israel and even on the journey itself.
Who does not need God's forgiveness for past sins? To obtain
atonement it is no longer possible to offer the sacrifices to God
in which the men of Israel once offered themselves to the Godhead
symbolically; but we can offer ourselves by joyfully exposing ourselves to the dangers of the journey and by gratefully accepting
death itself if it should overtake us.

At this point when the Rabbi's words have touched on the
boundaries of life, the Khazar intervenes with his second objection. He criticizes the Rabbi for having first expounded his
estimation of freedom to him and now proposing to take the
burden of new duties upon himself from which he is free outside
Palestine. In reply to this the Rabbi lays his fifth principle on the
table: what is supremely important is to free oneself from the
service of the many in order to serve the One. The service of
God is the true freedom, there is no other. Only the man who no
longer strives for the favour of men is entitled to court the
favour of God. This way, the way from dependence on human
favour to the free service of the merciful God is the true meaning
of the journey to the land of Israel.

Now the King brings forward his third objection, which
renews the main theme of the book, the distinction between
intention and deed: if the Rabbi holds all this fast because of the
reality of his faith then that is sufficient, for God knows his heart.
The objection seems strange. Has the Khazar forgotten what the
angel had revealed to him in the dream? Has he forgotten everything the Rabbi has taught him? On the contrary, he takes
all that as his point of departure: intention alone is not enough,
one must also be ready for action but if one is truly ready, if
one has overcome all the obstructions in one's soul, then one is

entitled to hope that God, in whose sight perfect spiritual readiness for action is equivalent to action itself, will accept the former with the same pleasure as the latter. The Rabbi replies to this with the sixth principle: readiness is equivalent to the action itself only when the action is impossible. For ' actions need completion '. After all, God also knows the thoughts of the person praying, yet they must be spoken with the lips in order to be regarded as complete prayer. God does not merely want the soul to be perfected, he also wants the world to be brought to perfection through the soul. He has created the world and man in such a way that the deeds of man can work towards the perfecting of the world into His Kingdom.

And from that the seventh and final principle, which elucidates and completes the first, concerned with the indwelling of the Shekhina in all pure hearts, follows on directly. The principle is that the action of those who make their way into the Holy Land with a ready soul will have its effect on the land of Israel, on the community of Israel, on the return of the Shekhina and on the Redemption. It is written in the Psalm: ' Thou shalt arise and have mercy upon Zion: for this is the moment to favour her, for the set time is come, for thy servants take pleasure in her stones, and favour the dust thereof.' (102, 13 f.) When the sons of Israel as God's servants, serving Him in freedom, shall be moved by a supreme desire for Zion and shall risk their lives for the fulfilment of their desire, then the ' set time ' will have come and Jerusalem will be built.

Everything has now been said that had to be said. The poet first made the Rabbi utter his own self-accusation, then his own decision and the reason for it. There, personal confession passed over into the interpretation of history, here it passes over into prediction. The prediction has the basic form on which all genuine prophecy is based, namely the form of ' If ', just as the interpretation of history had such a form, for it was also a prophetic interpretation. ' If we were ', thus the interpretation had run, ' ready with our whole hearts to meet the God of our fathers, we should obtain from him what our fathers obtained in Egypt '. What was prepared for in the ' If ' of the interpretation is now completed by the ' If ' of the prediction. ' Jerusalem ', so runs the prediction, ' will be built again, if Israel is seized by the supreme desire for it.' The speaker, the Rabbi—the speaker, the poet, is

seized by an extreme desire for it. He goes up there to fulfil his
longing and already senses in his own footsteps the footsteps of
Israel.

The fact that we only hear any more of Jehuda Halevi—
through his poems—from Egypt, Yemen, Damascus and Tyre,
and then no more at all, has the intensity of a symbol.

The Unfolding of the Mystery
(On the Book of Sohar)

THE ancient Oriental notion of the correspondence between the
heavenly and earthly abode of God acquires a special form in the
Haggadic notion of the 'upper' and the 'lower' Jerusalem. They
not merely correspond to one another, they are interrelated in a
mysterious way and interact on each other. This conception is
only fully developed, however, in the Cabbala. Here it is one and
the same essential substance that appears in heavenly and in
earthly form, seen first from the divine, and then from the human
point of view. Just as 'the Assembly of Israel', the power that
unites the people of Israel, is blended with the Shekhina, so too
'Zion' is taken up into the emanations of the divine substance
itself, without thereby losing its earthly reality. Within the cosmic
and supra-cosmic drama as which the Cabbala regards the process of all evolution, a special place is given to both the people
and the land, but above all to that which takes place between
them. To obtain a clear idea of this it will be sufficient to piece
together some characteristic passages scattered about the classical work of the older Cabbala, the 'Book of the Radiance'.

The idea that Jerusalem is the centre of the world, which fre-
quently recurs in Haggadic literature, is deepened here in a
peculiar way. Whilst there the notion of the world being centred
in Jerusalem represents merely a variant of a conception that,
without mutual interdependence, recurs in many cultures, a new
and transforming element is added here in that the centre in
space is interpreted with the strongest possible emphasis as the
beginning of time. The work of Creation begins with the heart
and the heart of the whole world is in the Holy of Holies in
Jerusalem where the Shekhina used to dwell and whence the
whole inhabited world is fed. Although the Temple has been

destroyed and the Shekhina, like Israel, is in exile, the earth still continues to be fed from this place, thanks to the powerfulness and worthiness of the 'good land'. But the heart itself is fed by the hidden brain of the world. The Temple, the Mountain of the Temple, Jerusalem, the inhabited earth and the ocean are founded on the Holy of Holies. But the same applies in the upper world, in the 'Mystery of the Upper King', where within the river of Fire circle upon circle is formed around the Holy City, in the centre of which the Holy of Holies is as it were the heart and through it everything else is fed by the upper, hidden brain. But both, Upper and Lower, are connected with one another and in their innermost essence they are not two but one.

The reason why God begins the Creation with Zion is that it is the sphere in which perfect faithfulness is consummated; therefore Zion is the heart of the whole world, the point from which it reaches its perfection.

This description of the Creation centred in Zion is supplemented, however, by another, a dualistic description in conformity with the drama of the cosmic struggle as seen by the Cabbala. According to this, the Creator divides the earth into the inhabited and the deserted part. The inhabited earth forms a circle, whose centre is the Holy Land, the centre of which is Jerusalem and the centre of which, in its turn, is the Holy of Holies on which the Blessing from on high pours down and from which it flows in all directions. But the desert is likewise laid out in circles around a centre; this is the desert of horrors, where the 'Other Side' has the seat of its dominion. And this is the desert through which Israel had to wander for forty years. If they had remained perfectly true to God during this time the 'Other Side' would have been obliterated from the face of the earth. Israel must do battle against demonry to obtain access to Zion; but what Israel succeeds in wresting from it will be for the benefit of the whole world, oppressed by the demonry.

From this point we can glimpse something of the importance of the connection between this people and this land as part of the world drama. The demonic force, the 'shell' that forms a crust round the delicate world brain, first grows out of a conflict which itself arises in the supra-cosmic sphere of pre-Creation in the upper worlds, it is strengthened and given bodily shape by

the rebellion of primitive man, and it is increased once again to
an extent, disastrous for the whole world, by the sin of Israel.
The effect of this sin is not limited to the human sphere, it extends
to the worlds and super-worlds. This sin, and likewise also the
atonement and redemption of Israel cannot be understood merely
as an earthly happening. Just as 'the Assembly of Israel', its
unity and its peace are bound up with the Shekhina, so the
inner contradiction of Israel, its dissension and decay are connected with the Klipa, the 'shell': what Israel does is done not
merely here, but also there, 'right' or 'left', what it suffers, leaves
its traces there too, every happening in the life of Israel affects
the spheres of the Emanation. But there is nothing in the life of
Israel, no action and no suffering in which the land is not
intimately involved, positively or negatively; Israel's sin is always
sin against the land, Israel's suffering always the suffering of the
land, Israel can be redeemed only along with and in union with
its land. Even though 'the heart of the world' is desolate and
the people that settled in it dispersed over a vast area, they are
still attached to one another and nothing can happen to the one
that does not happen to the other. But the participation of the
divine substance in the fate of the lowest of the worlds, our world,
is displayed in the vicissitudes of this relationship.

The importance of the land for man and his destiny is already
expressed in his creation, for 'man was created out of the dust of
the lower sanctuary'. The four elements and the four winds were
taken up into and mixed up with the dust; the perfect body was
formed from this mixture. The elements belong to the lower
world, the winds blow from the upper world, they intermingle in
the dust of Zion and in the human body formed therefrom.
Human sin acts on the earth of Zion and on all worlds. Israel is
destined to atone in Zion for man's sin.

It is Abraham in whom Israel emerges from the human race.
But he can only reach the high degree of nearness to God, for
which he is destined, in the land, it is only there that he can enter
into the covenant with God; even in its early ancestor Israel
can only attain that for which it is destined, through contact with
the land. In return, the holiness implanted in the land can only
develop through Israel's ascending the ladder of holiness; and
Abraham already knows that. But when he enters the land, he
learns still more. Here, in the middle of the inhabited earth he

stands confronted with a stern, impenetrable mystery. In each of the other lands which he passed through on his wanderings, he always soon discovered the power to which it is entrusted, the star by which it was governed. But here he is unable to find it, he is unable to 'get at the roots'. He perceives only one thing, that the whole world has been 'planted out' from this spot, but he is unable to perceive by himself the essence of this place. Then God 'shows' him the land, as he had promised he would when he sent him on his way. He shows him what the 'deep and hidden' power of this land is. It is the one power 'from which all the powers to which the other regions of the world are entrusted proceed and to which they are all attached'. It is well-known that God has appointed delegates to all peoples and lands; only the land of Israel is subject to no heavenly prince, to none of the angels, but to God alone. 'Therefore He brought the people that has no ruler beside Him, into the land that has no ruler beside Him'. Thus the Haggadic doctrine of the land's immediate relationship to God, of its independence of all subordinate powers, which is based on sayings from the Bible, is ingeniously inserted into the cabbalistic view of the world.

Abraham prepares the association of this people with this land for its cosmic and supra-cosmic task. What he has prepared is fulfilled when the Israel that has grown into a people comes into its land. Now everything falls into its proper place, the throne of Heaven stands intact over the people and the land, the divine office in the Sanctuary penetrates the ether and influences the upper spheres and from these the flow of blessing streams down unhindered on to the land and through the land into all the world. For the hard shell of deamonry which covers the delicate brain of the world has been pierced at this one point, it gapes, and in the Temple service the power of the upright people rises through the opening and rouses the counterstream of benedictory power. So long, therefore, as Israel leads a life devoted to God in its own land, the power of demonism is overcome and the Shekhina rules in the middle of the earth over a world open to the influence of grace.

But since Israel sins and desecrates the land, the two sides of the opening in the hard shell draw together until it is whole again and holds the brain of the world wholly in its embrace. Then the Temple is destroyed, Israel driven from its land and the

Shekhina itself goes into exile with it. Under the power of demon-ism foreign peoples gain domination over the land. Now the whole world stands under a curse, joy has died away in the lower and in the upper spheres.

Nevertheless, in the holy place itself in spite of everything the power of the demons cannot rule; here it still meets the limits of its power, here it still has no right to take what it likes. The Sanctuary lies in ruins, but God forbids the 'Other Side' to take possession of the Holy Place. Furthermore, after Israel has been driven out, the 'shell' is pierced again under the influence of grace. But as the holy people is no longer there for the power of its service to rise to heaven, a fine covering is laid over the open-ing, in order to protect the place and to prevent the hard shell closing in on it again. Now the flow of blessing can no longer pour down on the land and the ruined Temple cannot be rebuilt. But the power of demonry must also keep away. Thus, devastated and clouded over, and bereft of its people, the land remains in an intermediate state. The holy essence of ' Zion ' which had tarried in it was moved above in the hours of destruction and remains above in an intermediate state. But a change has also taken place in what was above : the upper Jerusalem, the Holy Land above, that is one substance with the Shekhina, has been lowered, separa-ted from God ; and only then was it possible for the earthly Jerusalem to be laid waste ; the upper Jerusalem also remains in the intermediate state, in ' exile '. In the world and in the super-world the centre of Being has been disturbed, the stream of divine power is at a standstill, confusion has come over the orders of heaven and earth.

Thus the great world drama is constructed around the histori-cal fate of Israel and Zion. The guilt of the people injures the life of the land and thereby the welfare of the whole world. From the expiatory punishment of the people intense suffering comes over the land and from the land over the whole world. The whole world stands under the curse that has befallen the people and its land. The demonry which had been overcome through Israel's rise to God returns to power through Israel's fall. In so far as the world drama is concerned not with pre-creation but with our world, Israel is the hero who sins and has to atone but his fate is transferred to the world and the super-world and thus appears to us in a cosmic and supra-cosmic setting and the fate of the land along with it. The disaster that has come upon the world derives from the fact that this people and this land are separated from one another. The disaster can only be overcome and the world can only find peace again through this people. But the people can only achieve what it has to achieve if it truly exists again, that is, if it is *one* again, ' *one* nation on earth' (11 Samuel 7, 23). So long as it is not one, God himself is as it were not one. But to become one again, the people must return from exile and dispersal into its own land, it must 'marry itself to this land'. At the right time God 'will raise the Assembly of Israel from the dust and make the world rejoice'. Then he will bring back Zion; it will come down again to its earthly habitation. The upper Jerusalem will be raised again to its original union with the essence of God and the power which unites them will flow again between Above and Below. The ' Other Side' will be wiped out and will vanish from the face of the earth and the power of God Himself will take the place of the hard shell, as it is written of Jerusalem : ' For I, saith the Lord, will be unto her a wall of fire round about' (Zechariah 2, 5). Then, as Israel will marry its land again, so the Holy One, blessed be He, will marry His Shekhina again, which is the Assembly of Israel. It is this whereof it is written (14, 9) ' In that day YHVH shall be One, and His name one '.

The world can be redeemed only by the redemption of Israel and Israel can be redeemed only by reunion with its land.

The Beginning of the National Idea

(On the ' high Rabbi Liva')

TWO hundred years before the French Revolution the basic rights of nations were expressed in a few clear-cut sentences which, in power and clarity of expression have not been surpassed since. They assert that every people has its own nature and its own form, that every people stands in its own power and ought not be subject to any other people, that every people has its natural dwelling-place and a right to live there, and it must be granted to every people to choose its own God according to its own way of thinking. But all this is not proclaimed as an agreed human statute, but as grounded in the order of the world itself, so that every trespass against it means a violation of the order of the world.

The man who first formulated these sentences was neither a statesman nor a political expert, nor one of the great teachers of natural and international law. It was Rabbi Liva ben Bezalel, the 'high Rabbi Liva' whom the legend of the Prague ghetto describes as the creator and master of the mysterious 'Golem' and of whom it is reliably reported that the Emperor Rudolf II summoned him, presumably to ask his advice about his experiments in alchemy. Rabbi Liva may be regarded as the real founder of a specifically Jewish philosophy of history, an attempt to understand the historical destiny of the people of Israel within a divinely directed world plan. Here the interpretations of the wanderings of the tribes and of the origins of the people of Israel, of the exiles and liberations of Israel, scattered in traditional writings, are pondered anew, reshaped from the depths and woven as never before into a unity, which has continued to exert its influence until the present day. To be sure, this unity was nowhere formulated systematically in the writings of R. Liva, not even in his main work, the 'Eternity of Israel', which was built up around the Messianic idea of history; but if one persists in searching for it in all his books, what one finds in all of them fits into an articulated religious interpretation of history unique of its kind. The statements on the basic rights of peoples shine through the structure in a simple but inclusive universality which is truly astonishing.

If one compares Rabbi Liva's doctrine of the nations with that of Christian thinkers, roughly from the beginning of the sixteenth to the middle of the seventeenth century, one realizes straight away that no one of them grasped the nature of national existence as he did. If we set alongside each other three representative systems of thought of three different generations of this period, that of Machiavelli, who died in R. Liva's early years, that of Calvin, who was born before him, and that of Grotius, who was twenty-five at the time of R. Liva's death, we find they all agree in regarding people and state as a unity; but within the unity, though in differing degrees, they show much greater interest in the state. To Machiavelli the nations are above all the populations of territories each of which possesses a special cultural unity but owes its real cohesion, in fact its very *raison d'être*, to its political or, if it has lost this in the course of history, its territorial unity. In Calvin's system the unity of the people as such is more prominent, it is true, just as he is, in general, nearest to R. Liva of all the thinkers in question : for him the decisively important fact is the divine election of collective entities and this is naturally concerned primarily with peoples, not with states. Here the Biblical idea of the ' holy people ' has been preserved; but for him a people can only fulfil its great religious tasks as a sovereign state,—this too is a result of his Old Testament thinking, but is exaggerated to a degree that it would be impossible for Jewish tradition and its representative R. Liva to accept it. For Grotius the importance of political existence within the life of the people is even greater than for Calvin, though not so great as for Machiavelli. He sees in national sovereignty the essential emanation of the whole unity of a people; if a people loses its sovereignty it loses its form. As against all these conceptions R. Liva affirms the nation as such, to which it is true that, so long as the world order is not disturbed, its own territory and independence do appertain, but which, if it has lost both, may be regarded merely as having fallen ill, as handicapped in its functioning, not as having been robbed of its essence and made incapable of fulfilling its specific tasks. Only a century after Rabbi Liva there arose a Christian thinker who, like R. Liva, based his conception of history on the existence of independent nations and who is also close to him, incidentally, in the fundamental distinction he makes between the history of Israel and that of the other nations; this is the founder of modern historiosophy, Giambattista Vico.

It is easy to understand how it came about that it was a Jew who was the first to formulate the basic rights of the nation as such. Here was a people that no longer enjoyed its own sovereign power but was subject to other peoples, that had lost its place on earth and had to live scattered over many lands and that was weakened and tormented because it remained faithful to the God whom it had chosen for itself. All this, the Jew realized, was against the order of Nature; it happened because the order of nature had been disturbed; but that order would be restored again. What all peoples enjoy must again be given to this one too. Liva ben Bezalel recognized as the basic rights of all peoples what his people, his people alone, lacked. Certainly there were—

our learned author was quite well aware of this—other peoples
in history whose independence had been stolen, whose land had
been laid waste and whose religion had been suppressed; but there
was none whose fate had robbed it of all rights whatsoever. It
was necessary to show, it was necessary to say, not, it is true, as a
warning to the other peoples, for their ears were out of reach,
but for the consolation of the Jewish people themselves, that
there are basic rights of nations, rights grounded in the order of
the world itself to which Israel has a claim like all others and
which God cannot, by virtue of the order He has Himself
ordained, withhold for ever.

It is true that, as the model of a nation chosen by God and as
the model of a nation which acknowledged God alone as its
supreme ruler, Israel was fundamentally important for the
Christian thinkers of the time, especially for Calvin. But their
attention was confined to the Israel of the Bible; they regarded
the quality of a chosen people and the principle of theocracy
as having passed from Israel to the Christian nations; the continuity between Israel and the Jews was hidden from the Christian eye, whereas for the Jew this continuity was of supreme importance, linking him up with the days of the Creation and the
days of the Messiah. Liva ben Bezalel's main concern was inevit-
ably to show that the Jews, in spite of all the defects of their
existence as a nation, were still the living people who at one time
had entered history, and that, as a living people, they were
entitled to all the rights of the nations.

Certainly, the essential thing about Israel for him was not
what it had in common with other nations, but what distinguished
it from them as a species of its own, its 'holiness'. For in the
very hour in which it became a nation the great name of God
was proclaimed over it: in its beginnings there was no time in
which it was just a nation and not also the people of God. Indeed, when it was created a people, it was already chosen,
for it had already been chosen in Abraham in a 'general', comprehensive and therefore indissoluble manner. But this uniqueness of Israel's was built up on the basic quality which it shared
with all other peoples, that of being a nation, and which con-
ferred on it the rights and privileges of a nation. The order of
election was erected upon the order of creation, to which the
creator had bound himself up to everything that was creation,—

and as one of the nations Israel belonged to the realm of Creation. R. Liva's doctrine of nations is founded on a rational system. In his exposition of the rights due to the Jewish people as to every other, he is a rationalist; where he reflects on what distinguishes this people generally from all others, he becomes an irrationalist. Israel has rights as a nation and only as a nation; Israel as Israel receives judgment and mercy.

' Every nation, says R. Liva, has two aspects, one as a people, and this aspect stands in the relation of matter, and one as a particular people, and this stands in the relation of form. ' Much as this follows the lines of the traditional Aristotelian categories, nevertheless it is aimed at the particular problem that is R. Liva's central theme. Considered materially—and we must take that as the starting-point—every people is simply a ' people ', that which is common to all peoples constitutes the ' matter ' of any people; but in each people this common 'matter' is wrought into that peculiar form by which the personal existence of the nation is constituted. It must first be established that Israel is a people, and all the relevant conclusions must be drawn from that fact; only then will one as it were be free to perceive what kind of a people this Israel is. Then one will be able to see that in spite of everything its nature and its ways are distinct from those of every other people; only then will one be in a position to recognize an origin, a destiny and a purpose which are so different from those of the other peoples that the differences between the latter are reduced to insignificance and only two finally confront each other : Israel and ' the nations of the world '.

' It is not seemly that one people should subjugate another '. ' It is not in accordance with nature and the order of the world that one people should be under another '. For 'every existence has its own strength since it is not seemly for any existing being to be in another's hands '. R. Liva stresses that this is ' a very great principle '. From this principle it follows that Israel's subjection to other peoples means a violation of the true order of the world, a breakdown in its health at this point. In its exile Israel itself is like a sick man who has left the natural human condition. This in itself already explains why the Shekhina, the indwelling glory of God is with Israel, as it is said in the word of God to the prophet (Isaiah 57, 15). ' I will dwell with him who is crushed and lowly in spirit ', for the essential abiding place of the

Shekhina is below. But if Israel does God's will, then—and only then—it is superior to all the peoples of the earth. This is truth of another sphere than that of the rational and rationally intelligible world-order: when the earth reaches up to heaven and makes the latter's will its own, the divine penetrates into the human.

'Man', says Liva ben Bezalel, 'chooses a godhead of whom he believes that it is his share'. Even when a people knows that there is a greater power than that represented by its own share of divinity, it still chooses its own nature as god. Not so Israel: it has made the absolute power, the God of all gods, its Lord. But, it must be added that it has forsaken Him. Whilst all the other peoples have held fast to the 'shares' which conform to their own nature, Israel has 'exchanged' the glory of the supreme God 'for that which doth not profit' (Jeremiah 2, 11). That explains its exile: the fact that Israel has disrupted the Order of election and revelation results in the disruption of the Order of Creation, of the creation of nations—Israel steps out of its natural state as a nation.

In his discussion of the relationship between Israel and its land R. Liva also takes the natural order of the world as his starting-point. Every people has its natural place. According to the order established by God every people's duty is to remain in its natural place; if it leaves it, then it cannot gain a footing anywhere else, for all other places are against and must remain against its nature. Only by returning to its own place can it find its way back again to the divine order. Israel's natural place, however, is 'the land of Israel'. Here too R. Liva encroaches on the irrational, though he bases his irrational reasoning on rational arguments. He teaches that to every person belongs the place which conforms to his nature, and to every people likewise; hence the Holy Land has been given to the holy nation. But this holiness of the nation can only be explained by the fact that, just as man was the last of the creatures to be created, so Israel was the last of the nations, and just as human nature cannot be deduced from that of other creatures, so the nature of Israel cannot be deduced from that of other nations. And yet Israel is a beginning, in fact the real beginning. The word 'beginning' has a double connotation, however. Even a kingdom which, like the fourth kingdom of Daniel's vision, intends to become all-inclusive so to make any reality outside impossible and which therefore destroys everything, may imagine that it is a beginning; that is why Amalek, God's arch-enemy, is called the ' beginning of the peoples ' in Bileam's prophecy: he is the foremost of all in that which differentiates the other peoples from Israel, in the mad, God-ignoring lust for power. Of Israel, on the other hand, Jeremiah says that it is consecrated to God and ' the beginning of his harvest ', and the Midrash rightly applies the opening words of the Bible ' In the beginning ' to this beginning: God created heaven and earth for the sake of this beginning, with the intention of creating this beginning. For the Messianic world-harvest is the goal of the seed of Creation and Israel is destined and called to become its beginning, dedicated to God, just as everyone in Israel dedicates the first-fruits of all his harvests, of every product of his soil, as an offering to God. R. Liva, however, advances still further in his combination of supra-rational and rational thinking. Every creature exists in the relative perfection of its specific kind; only the creature whose kind approaches perfection, is imperfect in its own kind. So it is with the Israelites who, more than all other nations, are the children of God: this supreme quality has not yet grown to perfection in them. In so far as they are imperfect in their perfect kind, they rank below the angels; yet their definite superiority is contained in their defect: in contrast to the angels, they can grow and as growing beings, as having the ability to grow to perfection they are nearer to God than the angels. But at the same time their guilt and their fate are conditioned by their defect. For those whose kind is imperfect are especially exposed to the temptations of Satan, above all when the kind in question is a high one,—for the higher the nature of a being and the more it deviates from the usual standards, the more easily the power that wills to destroy its nature fastens itself upon it, just as man is of all creatures especially liable to sin. Therefore in the hour after it had received the revelation and entered the highest stage of all, Israel lapsed into sin. It is this to which the Bible refers in the words: ' I have spoken: ye are gods and sons of the Highest ye all, but indeed, like men ye must die, ye must fall like anyone of the princes.' They have been punished more severely than any other nation just because of their holiness; for they have departed furthest from what is appropriate to their true nature.

In accordance with one doctrine of the tradition R. Liva interprets this punishment as purification. He sees it in two metaphors: the sufferings of the exile smelt the ore and separate the precious metal from the dross, they crush the olives and separate the oil from the waste. The transformation which takes place in this separation is aimed at overcoming the above mentioned defect: the imperfection of the perfect kind which has broken out into sin. Thus is the way prepared for Israel's rebirth. The hidden supreme power which longs to come to light is separated in the darkness of the exile from everything by which it is overcast and obstructed and grows into its perfect form. The extension of the ' vicious kingdom ' over the whole world is like the nine months of pregnancy. After this, the Israel will be born that is called ' Israel-Man '

Liva ben Bezalel does not shrink from considering this Messianic proceeding under the metaphor of Creation itself. All the destruction which has befallen Israel and its land precedes the new reconstruction, just as the creation of heaven and earth was necessarily preceded by chaos. Darkness covers the universe before the light is called into being.

Once again R. Liva sets out from the rational sphere in order to rise beyond it. As it is the inherent right of every nation to be free it cannot be robbed of its freedom for ever. That is grounded in God's relationship to the Order established by Him. 'He, blessed be He, who orders the whole of existence, it is impossible for anything to come from Him that deviates from His own established Order except for transient periods'. Thus R. Liva understands the Midrash interpretation of the word of God to Abraham (Genesis 15, 13): ' Know, know ': the Midrash explains that the first ' know ' means ' know that I shall enslave them ', but the second means ' Know that I shall redeem them ', An enslavement of nations by nations cannot endue for ever. And the same applies to the banishment of a nation from the natural place in which it is destined to live together in a settled community; it can only be temporary. ' Dispersion is not in accordance with the Order of the existing world, it is therefore not right that a homogeneous being such as Israel, which is a homogeneous people, should remain dispersed.' All natural things are essentially concentrated in themselves, all streams flow to the sea, and all dispersion tends towards collection. But the people of Israel is essentially less divided and less differentiated than all other nations; hence it is especially fitting that it should be gathered together in complete concentration. The saying ' All the people of Israel vouch for one another' refers to this special quality of unity ' which is to be found in no other nation '. Israel is like a man whose limbs all know when one of them is injured, for they are all One Body. That is why it is so all-important for Israel to maintain and strengthen its unity; for it is man's duty to co-operate with God. Dispersed among other peoples Israel is not regarded as a nation of its own, for a nation is something whole, whereas Israel only continues to exist, outwardly at any rate, as a collection of parts; therefore they must attend to the preservation and strengthening of their unity with all the power at its disposal and beware of all segregation. All the parts are liable to be influenced by the other peoples, they do not act, they are acted upon, for the part, which is forced to exist as a mere part, is weak and subservient, whereas the whole is strong and acquires independence by virtue of its wholeness. If Israel lives together in the true peace of all its parts, Satan, 'the power over non-being', cannot possibly attack it, for then Irael exists as a whole and undivided people in spite of the dispersal; but if it is at variance with itself, it only adds more division and dispersion to that already imposed on it. If Israel succeeds in becoming a really united people, then that in itself represents an exodus from dispersion and exile, an exodus before the exodus. But the power of concentration and unification is alive in Israel in the midst of the dispersion, R. Liva sees this power in the likeness of the arch-mother Rachel. She is buried not with the forefathers in the cave but ' on the road ': the unifying power remained with Israel in exile, certainly not in full actuality but potentially. From her grave on the road Rachel rises from time to time and pleads for mercy that Israel may be gathered together in its own land. Therefore God answers Rachel's complaint in Jeremiah (31, 16) saying that her children shall return to their own border. In the midst of the exile a unifying force is at work; for its sake Israel returns home. It is this unifying force that leads Israel to perfection; for through inward peace, *shalom*, one comes to perfection, *shelemut*. But it is also the unifying power that brings Israel into communion with God; for only if Israel is one in itself can it commune with God who is one in Himself. Then, when they are

together in a true covenant, all the different sections of the people
and human types in Israel all united into a single whole like the
four kind of plants in the sheaf at the Feast of the Tabernacle,
they will be gathered together and God will be raised over them
as their King.

According to R. Liva, however, Israel's original sin, which was
the first and decisive cause for the coming of the Exile, was the
people's refusal, after receiving the reports of the spies, to penetrate into the land of Canaan. The Exodus from Egypt is
'eternal', that is to say it is final and unalterable, for Israel's
relationship to God was born in its miracles. Not so the occupation of the land. It was originally intended that the Exodus from
Egypt and the entry into Canaan should form a single operation,
in other words, the generation that left Egypt was to be the one
entering Canaan. If this had been fulfilled, then the occupation
of the land will have been an eternal and irrevocable fact. But as
the people, instead of recognizing the land as its natural and
befitting place and yearning for it, refused to enter it, a contradiction arose between the originally intended and the actual
relationship of the people to the land. The result was that the
'coming' was no longer eternal: the possibility of exile which
had hitherto been excluded existed from now on. The weeping
of the generation of the wilderness resulted in the weeping of all
the generations of the Exile. It therefore depends on the relationship of the people to the land to what extent the originally
intended connection between the two can be realized.

The holy people and the Holy Land do in truth belong to one
another: both of them, the one as people, the other as land,
represent the centre of the world. R. Liva emphatically rejects
all theories according to which Palestine is central in the
geographical or astronomical sense, as contradictory to the
simplest cosmological facts, but he counters them with the
doctrine that it is the centre in an organic sense. If we speak of
the 'navel of the world', he argues, we have to remember that
the navel too is not the geometrical centre of the body but the
structural centre of its form. Palestine is in the centre of the earth
because it has the quality of a centre, that of being equally distant
from all extremes, from all 'ends'. Every extreme passes into
nothingness, for where it stands it contests Being as such, whereas
in the centre Being itself is concentrated above all ends. For that

reason the immigration into Palestine is called an ' ascent '. Concentrated Being is true life and that is why Palestine is called ' the
land of life '. But the people of Israel is also essentially medial.
Referring to Maimonides, R. Liva compares Israel to the central
shoot of the tree in contrast to the boughs and branches which
grow out to the side: they all tend towards different spheres,
each national branch towards the sphere of its own special
nature and special idea, whereas the central shoot which grows
from the main stem tends straight up towards the sky, bending
neither to one side nor the other. God has planted this people
neither with his right nor with his left hand but with both hands;
it is his own people. And so this people and this land
belong together from the beginning, by reason of their very
nature. In this sense, too, they are both ' set aside ': not in the
sense that they are separated from the rest of the world, but
for the world's own sake they persist in their medial existence,
in which they are interdependent and which they can only fulfil
together.

But of the two the land is the first and its influence is prior.
The high level of the patriarchs was reached through their connection with the land. ' If the land had not existed,' says R. Liva,
'the patriarchs would not have attained the supreme heights of
holiness and thus it was the land that made them great '. In the
patriarchs the essence of the land is shown forth in human form.
The land belongs to the forefathers to whom it was promised,
but the forefathers also belong to the land. Therefore Israel
possesses the land only if and so long as it is like the forefathers;
if it falls away from them and their standards, it no longer has
any hold on the land.

R. Liva compares the wisdom of Israel growing in its own
land with the wisdom of Israel in Babylon. The doctrine that
grows in Palestine does not depart from harmony, for in the land
that is the centre of the world everything is in harmony.
But Babylon is, in accordance with its origins, a mixture
without unity; therefore it is the home of sharp-wittedness
and disputation. ' In the land of Israel wisdom was acquired
with ease.'

But just as the land helps Israel to develop, so the land itself
receives help from Israel on whom, as long as it lives righteously
in the land, the Shekhina dwells. The land receives from the

people living on it both its life substance and its ' natural quality ';
it is thus that its holiness is achieved.

Since the people is in exile, the land waits for its return, in
order once again to receive both life substance and spirituality
from it and to renew its holiness. For ' the Romans have not taken
its holiness from Jerusalem ', they have not 'inherited' it; it has
only been ' lost ', it has only been ' laid waste '; in this condition
it waits for the people, in order to be renewed.

But even the people does not truly live without the land. Here
again Liva ben Bezalel links together the rational and the supra-
rational. The fact that Israel was enslaved in Egypt was a
necessary consequence of its homelessness; for unlike all other
peoples it had no domicile of its own and so the people were
born in a land that was not their own, as the slave is born in his
master's house. It was only when it came into its own land that it
was in its own might. There can therefore be no other liberation
for Israel but its homecoming. But because Israel is the holy
people it can not come to its own might except by coming into the
might of God; and because the land of Israel is the Holy Land,
Israel can only come into its own land by coming to God. The
purificatory effect of the Exile, the melting of the dross in the
furnace, the pressing of the oil from the olive, is purification for
the service of God. And the service of God by the nation as a
nation can take place nowhere but in the land of Israel.

The purificatory influence of the Exile is, however, also
directly purification for service of the land. In the midst of its
bondage in Egypt, Israel turns increasingly to its foundation, to
the soil, the people return to the soil with their souls and in their
way of life. Indeed, the compulsion of bondage helps towards this
process: the Egyptians force them into ' all manner of service in
the field ' (Exodus 1, 14) and so the shepherds learn to till the
soil again, as their fathers had done alongside their cattle breeding. With this turning to agriculture the nation enters deeply
into the life of nature; for man, Adam, has an elemental and
natural relationship to the soil, to Adama, which is his origin.
But the more deeply the people enters into the life of nature,
the more vehemently it longs for its land, the more seriously it
makes itself ready for the return to its own land and the nearer
it comes to it.

Every nation, Liva ben Bezalel teaches, is entitled to a land of its own in accordance with the order of the world. Thus the people of Israel also has a right to the land of Israel. The reason why God withholds it from Israel is not that it is less but because it is more than a nation: for in addition to being a nation it is also Israel. It is as Israel that the land has been given to it by God for the sake of Israel's special task: that of being the 'beginning of His harvest'. It is its own fault that it did not fulfil this task while it was living in the land. And because of this it has been exiled. But the land will be restored to the people as soon as it has been purified—and so will its task.

In accordance with the order of the world every people has a covenant with its land. So the people of Israel has a covenant with the land of Israel. But this is a covenant of a special kind, for it is a covenant between two 'holy' beings, in other words: of two beings each of which stands in a special and immediate relationship to God, in fact in a covenant with God. But this fact changes everything: Israel's destiny emerges from the daylight of the order of Creation into the mystery of the Revelation— into dark clouds and lightning. The dreadful and merciful God strikes in order to heal, burns in order to purify, and does not disturb the order of the world by His intervention.

A ZADDIK COMES INTO THE LAND

(On Rabbi Nahman of Brazlav)

IN Rabbi Nahman of Brazlav, the great-grandson of the Baal-Shem-Tov, the founder of Hasidism, everything was gathered together and concentrated, with and also without his knowledge, that the generations of the Diaspora had felt, dreamt and thought about the land of Israel. He must be seen as the great heir, who uses his inheritance magnanimously. It is characteristic of his nature and his mission that he became, without any literary ambitions of any kind, simply through oral intercourse with his disciples, the creator of a literary genre, the symbolical fairy-tale, but that in this new form age-old treasures of mystic tradition were assimilated and endowed with a supreme splendour. He is the best example possible of the relationship of the Hasidic movement to Palestine: everything flows together in him and everything finds exemplary expression in his life and words. But at

the same time we are aware of something else here, something
new, that seems to be connected in a strange fashion with our own
problems and struggles.

The Hasidic movement, which came to life somewhat suddenly
in Eastern European Jewry in the middle of the eighteenth
century, must be seen as the last intensive effort in modern
history to rejuvenate a religion. To judge merely by the degenera-
tion of the movement that has now been going on for more than
a century, it seems to have been a failure; but it has not merely
produced an abundance of splendid religious life and of its
transfiguration in legend, such as the world has only very seldom
seen arise from its midst, but it has also scattered seed in other
spheres some of which has already come up and the rest of which
will probably develop later on. Some day it will be impossible to
see and understand the best of what has arisen and is arising
now in the way of new human life in the Jewish settlement of
Palestine without connecting it with Hasidism.

The relationship of this movement to the land of Israel cannot
be reduced to a formula. It is only possible to do justice to it from
the point of view of its relationship to Messianism and this can
only be understood in its turn by taking into account the reaction
which followed the movement of Sabbatian heaven-storming.
Here the Messianic passion burst all bounds, people imagined
they saw with their own eyes and grasped with their own hands
the consummation of Creation, the renewal of all things, the
marriage of heaven and earth. The Law seemed to be abolished
in a changed world, and what had formerly been considered sin
not merely set free but sanctified. The collapse of the Sabbatian
venture signified the danger of spiritual destruction for a Jewry
whose soul had been kindled by its fiery breath. The danger
was directly perceived when Jakob Frank, the sinister epigone of
Sabbatai—one of the most interesting examples of the influence
which a man living in unrestrained self-deception is able to
exert in times eager for self-deception—swept crowds of Polish
Jews into his movement and into chaos. The Baal-Shem rises
against this threat of disintegration; he is the antagonist of the
fascinating lie. As such both he and his disciples have to try to
decontaminate the seriously diseased body of Messianism. The
feverish over-excitement of the hour has to give way to a
simultaneously enthusiastic and considerate contribution to the

cohesion of the times, the place of the unleashing of the instincts is taken by their sublimation (what is right in this concept of modern psychology is already expressed here in the clearest and most emphatic terms), and the daring incarnation phantasies are displaced by the quiet experience of intercourse with the divine in daily life. This naturally also leads to a change in the relationship to Palestine. Without losing the mystical luminosity which adhered to it from Talmudic times and had been powerfully developed in the Cabbala, the land is nevertheless stripped of the web of a slick magic which had entangled it in the period of heaven-storming. It is quite true that contact with the Holy Land is expected to prepare the way for redemption and that the legend bids Baal-Shem-Tov attach the highest possible hopes to a meeting that can only take place there; but at least early, classical Hasidism put an end to the ' pressing the end ' and the disciples of the founder and their disciples who settle alone or with a whole community of followers in Palestine are obviously thinking not of the unrepeatable miracle but of the continuity of the generations. The mystery has remained, but it has taken up its dwelling in the harsh reality of the tasks of daily life.

It is from here that even the founder's own attitude to Palestine is to be understood. We have little authentic knowledge of it or indeed of his life in general; but it is clear from the well-known letter to his brother-in-law who had settled there that he considered for a long time travelling to the Holy Land and had not given up the hope even then, about eight years before his death. Hints dropped by disciples of his indicate that he really did begin the journey on one occasion. Why he gave it up is not known. ' He was prevented by heaven ', the legend says, and the fact that it says so shows that a question to which the story-tellers sought to find an answer thrust itself on their attention at this point; in saying which we must note that the telling of this legend, however much apocryphal matter may have become attached to it later on, begins amongst the disciples themselves and in the third generation of Baal-Shem-Tov's own family, which had still known him personally. The various attempts of the legend to answer the question are characteristic. Already in his youth, when he was living with his wife in a hut on the slopes of the Carpathian mountains, dug clay and travelled to the nearest small town to sell it, a band of robbers whose quarrels

he was in the habit of settling is said to have offered to lead
him to Palestine through caves and subterranean passages; but
just as he was about to cross a deep bog with them on the way,
the revolving sword of the Cherubs is said to have appeared to
him and he had to turn back. At a later date (for it is said that
he was accompanied not only by his daughter but also, according
to another version, by her sons) he is reported by the legend to
have reached Istambul; here he was either warned in a dream
and bidden to return, or he embarked with his family and a great
storm broke out. At this point the stories part company again.
According to one version his daughter falls into the sea
from the battered ship, Satan appears and offers him his help but
he resists the temptation and decides to return home and immediately all danger is overcome. According to another version, he
lands on an island with a disciple where they are taken prisoner,
and both are afflicted with a numbness in which they even forgot
the words of their prayer; finally the disciple discovers that he
still knows the alphabet, he recites it to his master, who repeats it
after him ' with powerful enthusiasm ', and at once liberation
comes near and they return home. Similar things take place in
other versions. There is an unmistakable tendency throughout the
legend to warn against magical intentions in connection with
Palestine: so long as the hour of redemption has not arrived,
even the chosen are unable to conjure it up. This is a tendency
which is abandoned again in later Hasidism, or rather one about
which a violent struggle takes place; the Baal-Shem legend is still
unmistakably determined by it.

Nearly forty years had passed since the death of Baal-Shem-
Tov when his great-grandson made ready to travel to the Holy
Land. He was twenty-six at the time.

Here we are not dependent on the legend: his disciple and
apostle Natan recorded the journey step by step in accordance
with his own information; the ground we are on here is that of a
unique biographical interest that interprets some of the incidents
in legendary fashion but does not recast a single one.

Previously, before he makes known anything of his intention,
in fact apparently before it has ripened into a firm decision, he
visits his parents in Miedzyborz, which had once been the
domicile of Baal-Shem-Tov and where he had spent his own
childhood. Here something strange takes place. Once, when he

was a boy, he used to run to his great-grandfather's grave at night and ask him to help him to come near to God. But now, when his mother asks him when he intends to depart, he replies : ' If my great-grandfather wants to meet me, let him come here '. One can detect the fear lest the Baal-Shem, who was prevented ' by heaven' when he himself wanted to travel to Palestine, might oppose his intention. But in the night his great-grandfather appears to him and in the morning his mother knows it without his having to tell her. Later he only relates that he learnt from the apparition that he was to travel to the city of Kamieniec. Of his sojourn in Kamieniec it is reported that he spent the night alone in the city where Jews were forbidden to live and that thereafter the ban was lifted. He himself said later, whoever knows why the land of Israel was first in the hands of the Canaanites and did not come into Israel's hands until afterwards (' the skin had to precede the fruit', as he says in one of his didactic speeches) also knows why he was in Kamieniec before he travelled into the land of Israel. It was therefore a symbolical action that he stayed the night in the Jewless city, before he set out for the land promised to Israel, and it was precisely this action that he understood the Baal-Shem to have commanded him to perform. Before he set out for Miedzyborz, he had stated that he himself did not know whither he was travelling. By sending him to Kamieniec, his great-grandfather showed him the way he was to go.

On his return home he delivers an exposition on the Psalm verse : ' My soul has clung unto Thee, Thy right hand has held me up ' (Psalms 63, 9). The exposition has not come down to us, but we can guess the gist of it : He to whom his soul has clung from his childhood days—we know of the boy's tempestuous search for the favour of God—has now stretched forth His hand to support him. But at the same time his little daughter dies, and he connects this too with the new process that has begun; this too is strictly part of the context of the simultaneously wholly factual and wholly symbolical proceedings.

On the even of the Feast of the Passover he says, coming out of the ritual plunge-bath, to his attendant : ' In this year I shall certainly be in the Holy Land.' The speech which he makes on the Feast is based on the Psalm verse : ' Thy way is in the sea, and thy path in the great waters and thy footsteps are not known ' (Psalm 77, 19). Now they all know what he has in mind.

His wife tries in vain to persuade him to give up his plan. Who is going to feed his family while he is away? He replies that relations must look after them or they must go and work for strangers. He ignores the weeping all around him: whatever happens, he must travel—his greatest part is already there and the minority must follow the majority. He knows that he will encounter innumerable obstacles, but so long as there is breath in him he will risk his soul and go. At every step of the journey, he recounted later, 'I have risked my soul'.

In Rabbi Nahman's teaching as it has come down to us from later years we meet the 'Obstacles' in connection with Palestine again and again. The obstacles have, according to this teaching, a great significance. They are put in the way of the man whose yearning and destiny impel him into the Holy Land, so that he may overcome them. For they excite and exalt his will and make him worthy to receive the holiness of the land. Whoever intends to be truly Jewish, that is to say, to climb from step to step, must 'smash' the obstacles. But in order to conquer in this fight, 'holy boldness' is needed, the kind in which God delights, for He praises Israel because of the holy boldness and obstinacy of the Israelite man for the sake of which the Tora was given. This struggle is ultimately a spiritual struggle; for the powers of evil increase the obstacles in order to confuse the understanding, and fundamentally it alone is the source of the obstacles. But the greater a man is, the greater are the obstacles before him, for an all the more intense struggle is demanded of him in order to raise him on to a higher level.

After Nahman had announced his decision he seems to have been besieged with questions as to his reasons. Various answers have come down to us, as for example that he was concerned to amalgamate the commandments that can only be fulfilled in Palestine with the others, and to fulfil them first of all here, in thought, and then there in action; or that, after having now acquired the 'lower wisdom' here, he wanted to attain the 'higher wisdom' which can only be attained there. But the decisive motive is obviously to establish contact with a holiness which has its sole dwelling-place in Palestine, a contact by which one is enabled and authorized first there, and then here, to do mysterious works and to reach the summit of one's own vocation. In thinking of the greatness of the Holy Land,

one must not, he declared to his disciples later, long after his
return home, imagine a spiritual essence, something with which
it is possible to establish contact here: 'I mean,' he said, 'quite
simply this land of Israel with these houses and dwellings.' There
is an emphatic concreteness of feeling here in Nahman such as
we hardly ever find before him. Palestine as a concrete whole is
what is meant by the Holy Land. This holiness cannot, however,
be perceived from outside. In later years Rabbi Nahman tells of
what he heard from famous men who had immigrated only a
short while ago. They told him that before they actually got
there they had been quite unable to realize that the land of
Israel really exists in the world. From everything they had read
about its holiness in books they had imagined that it was 'a completely different world'. But when they came there they saw that
the land really does exist in this world, and in its outward appearance it is not different in kind from the other countries from
which they had come, its dust is like the dust of the whole world.
And yet the land is entirely holy. It is as with the true Zaddik who
likewise looks exactly like all other men. In truth, however, the
land is separate from other lands in every respect and even the
sky above it is different from the sky elsewhere. It is as with the
true Zaddik: only the man who believes in holiness recognizes
and receives it.

When all other arguments to persuade Nahman to abandon his
decision had failed it was pointed out to him that he had no
money for the journey. 'I shall travel immediately,' he replied,
'whatever the conditions, and even without money. Those who
take pity on me will give me something.' Now that they saw that
he was not to be held back, his relations collected the necessary
sum of money, and a week after the Feast of the Passover
Nahman departed with one attendant. When he was staying the
night in a certain place on the Sabbath, Rabbi Mendel of
Witebsk, who had gone to Palestine with three hundred trusty
companions twenty years previously and had died there ten years
ago, at the beginning of this very month, appeared to him in a
dream. As a boy he had even visited the Baal-Shem. Stories about
him and his own statements agree in establishing that he continued Baal-Shem's fight again the Messianic fever both before
his journey to the Holy Land and in the Holy Land itself. The
story is told that when he was staying in Jerusalem a foolish man

had, without being noticed, climbed the Mount of Olives and
blown on the ram's horn which is the sign for the beginning of
the world and said : ' There is no renewal.' His companion, Rabbi
Abraham of Kolisko, gives those who have remained at home
information about the many ' changes, revolutions, events and
time sequences ' through which every individual in the land
must pass ' until he is a real part of it and delights in its stones
and feels kindly towards its dust and loves the ruins in the land of
Israel . . . until the days of his resorption are over and he is fully
resorbed into the life. . . . Everyone who comes to the Sanctuary
must be born again in his mother's womb, be suckled again, be
a little child again and so on, until he looks directly into the face
of the land and his soul is bound up with its soul.' Rabbi Mendel
himself writes to those who have remained at home : ' My dear
ones, my friends and companions, know truly that I know perfectly clearly that all the sufferings which we have passed through
in these three years are the sufferings of the land of Israel ', that
is to say, they are part of the sufferings which are, according to
the Talmudic tradition, necessary in order to acquire the land;
they are therefore of precisely the same kind as the ' obstacles '
which Rabbi Nahman interprets. This is the man, therefore,
who appears to him in the first night of his journey. He reveals to
him that on a sea voyage the divine name of ' Thou ' must be
called upon : He will overcome the waves, as it is written in the
Psalms (89, 10) : ' Thou rulest the swelling of the sea; when its
waves rise, Thou calmest them '.

He spends the Feast of the Revelation in Cherson, on the
journey to Odessa. A speech which he makes here obviously links
up with the communication which he received in the dream; it
is based on the Psalm verse : ' He maketh the storm a calm so
that the waves thereof are still ' (Psalms 107, 29). On the eve
of the Feast, after his usual vigil, he goes into the plunge-
bath with a companion. On the way he asks him time after
time whether he cannot hear the sound, the man denies it,
finally Nahman says : ' It may be coming from a band '. But
the man understands : The Rabbi has heard the thunder of
Sinai.

The sea-route via Odessa had hitherto been avoided by the
Jews as dangerous. He undertakes it and from then on it seems
safe to everyone. It often happened like this in his life, we are

told: he draws the poison-fangs from the things that he is the first to dare to endure.

As soon as the ship is on the high seas, a storm breaks out, water floods the deck. In the great storm Nahman sees a young man coming towards him who had recently died in his home district and hears him entreating him to bring redemption to his soul. That is the first of very many souls who appear to him in this way.

In Istambul troubles and hardships increase. Nahman forbids his companion to say who he is. He not only has to suffer at the hands of the Turkish officials—it is the period of Napoleon's Egyptian expedition, and the fear of spies is great—but he is even suspected and insulted by the Jews; he keeps nevertheless to his disguise, not merely endures the abuse but even provokes it deliberately and contrives to increase it. If, he says to his disciples in a later period, he had not experienced all the humiliation, then he would have remained in Istambul, in other words, he would have had to die there. ' Before one achieves greatness,' he says, ' one must first descend to smallness. But the land of Israel is the greatest greatness, and that is why one must go down into the smallest smallness before one can rise up to it. That is why the Baal-Shem-Tov was not able to reach there for he was unable to descend to such smallness.' But he, Nahman, makes himself small. He goes around in Istambul with bare feet, in a loose coat of coat-lining without a belt, without a hat over his skull-cap, and perpetrates all kinds of tomfoolery; thus he organizes with several other people war-games in which one side represents the French and the other those attacked by them. This making himself small and acting the fool, which reminds us of Buddhist, Sufic, and Franciscan legends, establishes itself so firmly in him that later on, in Palestine itself, he finds it difficult to get rid of the habit.

In Istambul the plague breaks out. For a long time he is unable to travel on. On account of the approaching danger from the French the Jewish community forbids all indigenous and foreign Jews to leave the city by sea. Nahman resists the prohibition and induces many to travel with him. On the journey a great storm breaks out again and the ship is threatened. All are weeping and praying but he remains seated and silent. People question and press him in vain; at first he makes no reply, then

he scolds them : ' Keep quiet, all of you! As soon as you are
quiet, the sea will also quieten down '. And so it happens. After
further troubles—the drinking-water gives out—the ship comes to
Jaffa. Rabbi Nahman intends to go on to Jerusalem from here,
for the Holy City is the goal of his desire—he explains explicitly that he does not want to go either to Safed or Tiberias,
where the Hasidic groups have settled—but the harbour authori-
ties suspect him, on account of his conspicuous appearance, of
being a French spy and forbid him to land. This takes place two
days before the high Feast of the New Year. The captain means
to stay some days outside Jaffa, but the ship cannot anchor
because of the rough sea. In reply to his questions, the wise men
of Sephardic Jewry tell the astonished captain that according to
an oral tradition the prophet Jonah was once thrown into the
sea in this place; this is believed to be the reason why a ship
is sometimes prevented from riding at anchor here. They travel
on to Haifa and anchor the evening after at the foot of Carmel,
opposite the cave of the prophet Elijah. In the morning the
prayers are said on the ship, then the Jews go on land, Rabbi
Nahman among them.

In later times he tells his disciples that as soon as he had gone
four ells in the land, he had already brought about all he had
striven for. In this report the belief in the power of *contact* with
the holiness of this land becomes particularly clear. What he
means is explained by another statement about what he had
achieved which he made soon after his return from Palestine
and which is to be compared to that on the amalgamation of the
commandments which are destined for the Holy Land with the
other ones. He said that he had now fulfilled the whole Tora
in every way, 'for I have attained the fulfilment of the whole
Tora, and even if I had been sold to the Ishmaelites in distant
lands, where there are no Jews, and had been put there to graze
cattle, and even if I had then no longer known the times of the
Sabbath and feast days and had no longer had either prayer-
mantle or prayer-strap and not any commandment I could
accomplish I should have nevertheless been able to fulfil the whole
Tora '.

In the afternoon—it is the even of the New Year—they go into
the plunge-bath and afterwards into the house of prayer where
they stay until the evening. ' Blessed art thou,' Nahman says to

his attendant on his return to the inn, 'that thou wast judged worthy to be with me here.' He has the names of all the Hasidim read aloud to him, who had joined him at home and had given him slips of paper with their names and the names of their mothers, so that he might remember them in the Holy Land, and he thinks of each one of them in his great joy.

But on the morning after, his feeling has changed. An unspeakable anxiety has been aroused in him, his heart is oppressed and he speaks to no one. Immediately after the feast he thinks of the return journey. He does not even any longer want to go to Jerusalem, he wants to go back to Poland. From Safed and Tiberias come invitations of the Zaddikim, who have heard of his arrival, to spend the Feast of the Tabernacle with them but he ignores them and remains for both the Day of Reconciliation and the Feast of the Tabernacle in Haifa.

And now something happens which is indeed not very remarkable in itself, but becomes remarkable through the way in which first Nahman himself, and later his disciples, to whom he relates it, regard it. Day after day a young Arab comes into the inn when the Rabbi is sitting at his midday and evening meal, sits down beside him and keeps on talking to him, kindly but insistently, tapping him on the shoulder between times and showing him his goodwill in every conceivable way. Nahman naturally does not understand a word of what he is saying, and the demonstrations of love make him pretty uncomfortable, but he does not express any impatience and remains seated as if he were listening. But one day the Arab returns, armed and angry, and marches violently up to the Rabbi who naturally again does not understand a word. Only after the Arab has departed does he learn that he had been challenged to a fight. Nahman is hidden in the home of another Zaddik. The Arab comes to the inn again and is beside himself when he hears that the man he is looking for has escaped him. 'God knows', he solemnly declares, 'that I love him dearly. I want to give him a donkey and my own horse so that he can go to Tiberias with a caravan'. Nahman then returns to the inn. The young Arab comes again, but now says not a word, he merely smiles at the Rabbi from time to time. Apparently he also fulfils his promise. Evidently he was only concerned to hire the animals—we can explain the happenings related in this way—and as the Rabbi appeared to listen to him, he felt offended because he did not accept his often repeated offer; in the end the situation was cleared up and when he looked at Nahman he had to laugh. In a statement that has come down to us, the Rabbi said that he had suffered more from the Arab's love than from his anger. But beyond that he seems to have dropped a few hints about the mysterious danger that lay behind this episode, and the pupils understood him to mean that the Arab had been Satan in person. We here gain a particular insight into the symbolically legendary way in which Nahman experiences his life and in which his disciples learn of it from his report and work it up into the story that has come down to us. The Arabian donkey-hirer becomes the Satanic embodiment of the ' obstacles'. This is given as the explanation of the melancholy that the Rabbi experienced before the conflict.

Meanwhile Nahman allows himself to be persuaded to undertake the journey to Tiberias, where he falls ill—once again an event of symbolical significance. Then we hear of an informer whose designs he frustrates. Visits to some caves of holy men are reported with a few legendary touches. Thus he is said to have visited a cave with the tomb of a holy child, which had hitherto been shunned on account of a snake that was supposed to reside there; when he came, no snake was there, and from then on everybody visited the cave. Here too Nahman appears as the forerunner, the pioneer.

One of the great Jews of Tiberias presses him to reveal to him the hidden purpose of his coming to Palestine. Obviously, he said, the Rabbi was concerned to perform a secret action in the service of God; if he would only tell him what it was he would assist him to the limit of his powers. When Nahman refuses, he asks him to make known something of his teaching to him. But as soon as he begins to tell him the secret of the four points of the compass in the land of Israel, blood rushes out of his throat and he has to break off, for ' heaven does not agree'.

In Tiberias the plague breaks out. Nahman makes his way on subterranean paths through a cave and not without danger, to Safed. Attempting to find place on a ship for the return journey, he comes with his attendant on to a Turkish warship, which they take for a merchantman. They discover their mistake too late. After undergoing severe hardships and all kinds of

adventures they reach Rhodes where they celebrate the Feast of
the Passover. From there they travel by way of Istambul and
Wallachia. Here the Rabbi speaks on the Sabbath at the holy
Third Meal about the verse of the prophet Isaiah : ' When thou
passest through the waters—I [= I am] with thee ' (43, 2). This
speech closes, in the version that has come down to us, with the
words : ' I with thee—see that thou becomest the tool that is
called I '. This is what he wants to declare of himself in this
hour : that on his journey over the water he has become the tool
called I.

This enables us to understand what he henceforth, in the
time—not much more than a decade—which still remained of
his life and in which he built up his teaching and writing, reports
to his disciples again and again, if only in hints, of what he had
acquired in the Holy Land. Thus he relates that before he
' six hundred thousand ' letters of the Tora surrounded him as
if the Tora had broken up again into an uncontrolled pro-
fusion of letters; but since Palestine this disturbance has
ceased and he has the whole of it in his mind in such
a way that it is impossible for it to split up and become
chaotic. Or : in his youth he was often overcome by violent
tempers and he fought against them; but to break a bad habit
does not mean that it has been completely overcome; on the contrary, the whole force of the passion at work in it must be transformed into good : he had only succeeded in this—no longer
merely not hating, but loving what previously seemed hateful
with all the passionateness that had previously gone into the
hatred—in the land of Israel. And the same is true of the teaching. Between the doctrines which come from outside Palestine
and those which come from Palestine, he says, there is a
difference as great as that dividing East and West.

Statements that he made nine weeks before his death on the
eve of the Sabbath after the Mourning on the Ninth day of the
month Ab, the day of the destruction of the Temple, give an
even deeper insight into the transformation that he owed to the
land. Shortly before, he had moved into a new house, his last,
where he looked out from the window on to a garden and,
beyond that, the cemetery—with the graves of the thousands who
had perished in the great Cossack massacre ; he looked at it again
and again and said how good it would be to lie among the

martyrs. This was the first discourse in the new house. Many Hasidim, from long-standing intimates to those who had only just joined him, were gathered together as he entered and performed the consecration of the wine. It was obvious that he was very weak and hardly had the strength to speak. Afterwards he did not return to his room as was his usual custom, but remained seated at the table. Very feebly he began to speak. ' Why do you come to see me? ' he said, ' I know nothing now, I am now a simpleton.' This he repeated time and again. But then he added that he was only holding on to life because he had been in the land of Israel. And as soon as he had said this, his teaching power arose within him again, the enthusiasm overcame him, and he began to speak of the fact that vital force flows into all the simpletons in the world from the Zaddik's condition of simplicity, for everything is interconnected. But the source of this vital force is in the land that was the land of grace even before Israel entered it with the revelation of the Tora, the ' treasury of the undeserved gift '. It was from here that the world was preserved between Creation and Revelation, here the doctrine of God was hidden, the Ten Words of Sinai in the Ten Words with which the world was created, and this is the teaching in which the fathers lived in the land. It is called Derekh Erets, the way of the earth, in other words, the right way of life outside Revelation, and indeed it is the way to the earth, to the land. Since the power of the Ten Words of Creation is hidden in the land and the fathers have lived in the strength of the Ten Words, Israel, to whom God ' proclaimed the power of His works ', as ' to His own people ', was able to come into the land with the Ten Words revealed to them. Thus Israel's appropriation of the land is the encounter and association of Creation and Revelation. In order to prepare the way for it, Canaan first had to be in the hands of the heathen, before it fell to the lot of Israel; but that is precisely why the peoples cannot say to Israel: ' Ye are robbers, in that ye have conquered a land that does not belong to you.' Admittedly this is only so as long as Israel merits this exceptional consideration, so long as it hallows the created earth with the holiness of the revealed Tora which it fulfils and is allowed to remain in its land; as soon as Israel has to go into exile, the land enters once again into the state of the hidden doctrine, of the Ten Words of Creation alone, of the undeserved gift, of pure grace. The

Zaddik lives on this strength of the land when he falls into the state of simplicity and from there the vital force streams into him which flows from him to all the simple-minded in the world, not only of Israel but of all peoples. This is precisely why he has occasionally to fall for a time into this state of simplicity. Thus even in the deepest sinking there is the hidden purpose of an ultimate rising. And thus it is in some measure and some way for all men, for the men of spirit as well as the simple : from none is the source of life withheld unless he himself withdraws from it. Therefore the most important thing is not to despair.' There is no such thing as despair !' cried Rabbi Nahman. ' One must not despair ! I implore you, do not despair !' A great joy had been kindled within him. Before they washed their hands before the meal he bid them strike up the song, ' I will sing praises ', that was not usually sung until after the blessing, and had not been sung at all since he had become so weak. ' Strike it up, Naftali,' he said to a pupil. When the latter blushed and hesitated, he cried : 'Why should we be ashamed? The whole world was created for our sake ! Naftali, why should we be ashamed ?' And he himself joined in the singing. ' Thus we have seen ', the disciple writes in his narrative, ' how God's concealment is trans-formed into grace. From a state of ignorance the Rabbi has arrived at such a revelation. He himself said that his ignorance was more remarkable than his knowledge.'

Rabbi Nahman did not travel to Palestine for a second time. Three years before his death he said that he had wanted to go there to die, but he had been afraid that he might die on the way and then no one would come to his grave and tend it. ' I want ', he said on another occasion, ' to remain among you.' But Palestine permeated everything in his mind. ' My place ', he used to say, ' is only the land of Israel. If I travel anywhere I shall travel only to the land of Israel.'

When he spoke of the holiness of the land, he sometimes fell into such deep ecstasy that he came near to dying.

Rabbi Nahman of Brazlav is one of those Hasidim who, like Rabbi Mendel of Vitebsk and his companions, hint at the resettle-ment of the land by their own settlement in Palestine. In this respect he does not, as in the fairy tales he told, introduce a new era. But as the great heir that he is, he melted down all the traditional material into his glorification of the holiness of the land and reshaped it. No one in the whole of Jewish literature has ever praised it so manifoldly and so uniformly at the same time.

According to Rabbi Nahman, Palestine is the starting-point of the creation of the world, its foundation-stone, and it is the source of the coming world in which everything will be good. It is the real centre of the spirit of life and therefore the renewal of the world by the spirit of life will also proceed from it. The spring of joy, the perfection of wisdom and the music of the world is in it. It represents the covenant between heaven and earth. The perfecting of faith proceeds from it, for here one can give oneself up wholly to the infinite light as nowhere else in the world and be illuminated by it; from it there proceeds the setting right and perfecting of justice in the world, and the overcoming of anger and cruelty. It is the place of peace in which the antitheses of grace and power are united and the unity of God is revealed; it is here that peace is established in the human heart, ' between his bones ', between man and man, and from here peace goes out into the world. Rabbi Nahman adopts the Talmudic teaching that all other lands receive the heavenly plenty through messengers, through the ' princes of the upper sphere ', but that Israel receives it directly from the hands of God Himself: that is why it is so difficult for the other peoples to advance to unity, whereas Israel is embraced as a unity by the dictum ' Thou art one ' and from Israel unity is to come over the whole world of man. Therefore the land of Israel is as it were the Shekhina, the ' indwelling ' of God Himself.

The land is the highest of all lands, but it is also the lowest of all. Canaan means ' submission ', as it is written: ' And the humble shall inherit the land.' The highest land submits itself in the deepest humility and its very dust teaches the lesson of humility. Therefore the resurrection of the dead will have its centre here. But for the same reason Israel has not yet regained the land. ' Because of pride we have not yet returned to the land.' It is particularly stressed that it is not because the others are so many but on account of their own ambition and haughtiness that the Jews cannot get back to their land. The obstacle is in themselves.

But the dust of the land of Israel has a ' magnetic ' power too: it draws men to holiness. There are two opposite kinds and powers of dust: the dust of the land of Israel, which attracts men to holiness, and an impure counter-dust which attracts them to the 'Other Side'. But this 'counter-dust' takes on the same appearance as the pure dust and behaves as if it were the dust that attracts men to holiness. ' For in this world everything is mixed up and confused.' But in reality it is nothing but an ensnaring and entangling constraining power. This is the ' dust of the Other Side'. In the language of today : the power of the earth over man is twofold. The earth can exert a healing influence on the man who settles on it and serves it, by binding him to its indwelling holiness, and then the spirit of man is supported, strengthened and borne by the power of the earth; but it can also pull man down and stir up his powers of imagination against the spirit; it can deny and renounce the higher powers and assign all power to itself. In the nature of the earth as everywhere in the world, purity and impurity, consecrating and desecrating influences confront each other. But the pure and healing power of the earth is represented in the land of Israel.

We have heard that the resurrection of the dead will have its centre in the land of Israel. That is why the tomb achieves its perfect form here ; here alone is the place of perfect burial. For the reason why death has been imposed on man is known to tradition : it is because in the sin of the first man a defilement by the serpent invaded our imagination from which we can be perfectly cleansed in no other way than by the death of the body. In a proper death and a proper burial the impurity is dissolved and a new body will arise in a renewed world. All this, however, is perfectly achieved only in the land of Israel. For the overcoming of the defiled imagination occurs through faith, but the power of faith has implanted itself in this land and lives and works therein. Abraham, the father of faith, was the first to reveal this holy power when he acquired the burial-place of the cave of Makhpela.

Here, in the land of Israel, the purification of the imagination through faith takes place. It is not for nothing that the sounds of the words *adama*, soil, and *medame*, imagination, resemble one another : the fullness of the elements comes to the imagination from the earth. But the purification of the imagination by faith can also take place in no other way than through the consecrated earth and the consecrated earth is here, in the land of Israel. Everywhere else the sparks of faith have fallen into the

confused imagination which is overlaid by the earth. Therefore
it is already written of the fathers (Exodus 13, 17) that ' God led
them not through the way of the land of the Philistines, although
that was near ', but ' God led the people about ' : in order that
they might take care of the sparks of faith dwelling everywhere
and to purify the imagination in all the places through which
they pass. In this way a man becomes worthy of receiving the
perfection of the purified imagination and the perfection of faith
in the land of Israel.

All this, however, both the significance of the holiness of the
land and the difficulties which rise up before the man who really
wants to attain it, must be grasped at a still deeper level.

Because here in the land of Israel faith has the place of its perfection, because here in very truth is ' the gate of heaven ', in
which the upper and lower spheres meet and one can enter
here from the outside into the inside and those who stand outside can join up with those inside, hence ' the perfection of all
worlds and the perfection of all souls ' proceeds from here. For
this perfection develops from man's utter surrender to the light
of the boundless, but this can only happen here, nowhere else
can man receive and absorb the light with his whole nature. For
this to come about, however, it is necessary that the vessels shall
first be perfected in order to receive the light. And again only
the holiness of the land can bring about the perfection of the
vessels. That is why it is so difficult to get there for those who
want to attain the holiness of the land. The former depends on
the latter and the latter on the former. How is one to get out of
this vicious circle ? The greater the one, the greater the obstacles.
That is why whoever stakes his soul to reach the land, breaks
through the vicious circle, for the light of the holiness of the
land streams towards those who still stand outside and gives them
the strength to break the obstacles, the demonic ' shell-powers '.
The vessel is perfected and gives itself up, service in the cause
of the perfection of all worlds and all souls takes place.

When the sons of Israel adopted the Tora and came into the
land, they were allowed to raise its holiness from obscurity into
the light of day. When they transgressed against its manifest
holiness, by not fulfilling what was revealed to them, and finally
had to leave the land, its holiness fell back into obscurity again
and has lived and worked there ever since. ' The land of Israel

still continues in its holiness out of the power of the hidden Tora and undeserved grace. And therefore we are always on the look-out for a chance to return to our land. For we know : although it is in great seclusion the land is still ours even now '.

Even though the ' other side ' has robbed Israel of its land, it proclaims its protest in the power of prayer. It cries : ' The land is ours, for it is our inheritance.' And so long as it proclaims its claim to the land, according to divine law the appropriation of the land by the ' other side ' is no authentic appropriation. But how is the land to be regained? Everyone from Israel has a share in the land, everyone from Israel can have a share in its redemption. According to the measure in which he purifies and sanctifies himself, so he will be judged worthy to seize and conquer a part of the land. The holiness of the land can only be conquered gradually. But since this part must take place in the whole of life, in every action and in every domain, it is right that man should withdraw from the learning of the Thora from time to time and concern himself with the 'way of the earth', as the wise men say.

Those, however, who have been judged worthy to settle in the land of Israel, are to remember at all times the great radiance and illumination that went forth from the land in early times and are to remember that holiness is eternal. And even when its illuminating power seems to have disappeared, a holy trace of it remains. With its eyes fixed thereon, Israel hopes and waits at all times for a ' new light to shine on Zion '.

This land is a small, humiliated land—yet the hope of the world is contained within it. Whoever settles in it in truth, so that he has intercourse with the holiness of the land and helps it to prepare the way for the redemption of the world, into his apparently poverty-stricken life there streams the glory of the higher spheres, yearning for union with the lower. He eats ' bread with salt ', as recommended by the wise men as ' the Way of the Instruction ', but this bread is in fact the very bread of the land and the grace of faith is harvested, ground, and baked into it. ' In the land of Israel the bread is so tasty that it contains all the pleasant tastes of all the foods in the world. As is written : " Thou shalt not eat thy bread in indigence, it shall not lack anything." '

In one of his tales Rabbi Nahman tells of a simple shoemaker who eats dry bread for his midday meal, first as a spicy soup, then as a juicy roast and who ends by enjoying it as a delightful cake : he lacks nothing. Does his imagination deceive him as to the poverty of his existence or does his faith not rather enable him to taste in the divine food what lies hidden therein ? Nahman, who like all genuine masters of the Hasidic doctrine praises the wisdom of simplicity again and again, points out that the patriarch Jacob who was given the land of Canaan for his own (he is the real receiver among the patriarchs, because none of his sons must be excluded but together they already represent the people of Israel), is called a ' simple man '. Of the land of Israel itself Rabbi Nahman says that it represents simplicity. That means, however, that it represents the true wisdom. For it is the true wisdom to taste in one's bread all the pleasant tastes of the world and it is the true wisdom to recognize the gate of heaven in the poor and sterile little land.

PART FOUR

THE ZIONIST IDEA

THE ZIONIST IDEA

THE FIRST OF THE LAST
(On Moses Hess)

IT IS well known that Moses Hess is the founder of the modern Zionist system of thought. But, in spite of Herzl's statement that 'everything that we have attempted is already present in his work', it has not yet been sufficiently observed that there is not a single leading principle in this system that is not already outlined in Hess' *Rome and Jerusalem*. This work cannot be called a good book, it is formless and careless, but it is the book of the pioneer. However often one reads it, one is always surprised anew by the phenomenon of this man who goes along as it were with a divining-rod finding veins of gold. A long time passed before his ideas were taken up and thought out to their logical conclusion and even today some of them have not yet been given their full due. In this first pioneering effort a bold intellectual initiator succeeded in penetrating to the very heart of the Zionist idea.

How did the socialist Hess arrive at this glorification of the unity of the people and the land? Behind this question another lies hidden: how did this man, who in his socialistic writings never reached the heights of the crucial, forceful word, reach them here?

An important Marxist thinker of our time, Georg Lukács describes Hess as a completely wrecked forerunner of Marx, whose fate must be considered tragic since he was not only personally a thoroughly honest revolutionary but because 'of all idealistic dialecticians he sometimes came nearest to the Marxist version of dialectics', and he explains the 'failure' in more detail as follows: 'As a theorist he was brought to ruin by his contact with materialistic dialectics.' But no matter whether this sentence is true as far as Hess the socialist is concerned, it is certainly not true of Hess the Zionist. A man who, fifteen years after he had acknowledged the materialistic dialectic, expressed such independent and mature thoughts as in *Rome and Jerusalem* and the supplementary writings, was not wrecked and was not ruined. With Hess the way to the knowledge of living Judaism and its task is also the way of ascent of his own personality. And yet this ascent can only be understood by a consideration of Hess' contact with the materialistic dialectic.

Hess became acquainted with Marx in 1841 and was immediately fascinated by him; in a letter to Berthold Auerbach he calls him his 'idol'. We can guess what it was in Marx that made such an impression on him: the strictness of his thinking, the stern coherence of the thoughts, disciplined from the very start, the inexorable consistency, in a word, the well-organized mind. Hess himself lacked such qualities. He had genuine ideas, born of genuine meditation, but not one of them led to uniform equally valid inferences, not one grew into a great, concentrated intellectual structure. From the very beginning Marx's thought was exclusive, it shut out whatever did not fit into it, and thus developed into that unprecedented force which has continued right up to our own time to give the masses the belief in the identity of their will with historical necessity and has thereby inspired them to a period of unheard-of activity. Hess' thinking was essentially inclusive; unlike Marx he did not renounce nature in favour of history and ideas in favour of economics; he wanted to embrace both and yet was unable to, he did not attain a synthetic mastery of his problems and is therefore numbered among the 'failures', about whom, however, the last word has not yet been spoken.

The years which followed Hess' meeting with Marx are those in which Marx's materialistic conception of history matured; for Hess, by whom he was not inconsiderably influenced, they are the years of inner resistance against this conception. Much as he recognizes the importance of social conditions for the development of social ideas, he nevertheless considers it essential that socialism should be based not on the economic and technical stage of development alone but also on that of the spirit. For him social freedom is 'either a result of spiritual freedom, or it is without foundation and turns over into its opposite'; he sees the heart of the social movements of our time proceeding 'not from the needs of the stomach but from the needs of the heart' and from 'ideas'. But he is not able to enlarge this—from Marx's standpoint 'utopian'—independent view of his independently, he is incapable of building it up into the foundation of a socialism

valid for the coming generations of the proletariat and he himself becomes aware of his inability to do so. About a year after
Marx had recorded the mature formulation of his conception for
the time being in aphoristic form in the *Theses on Jeuerbach*,
about the same time as Marx and Engels had completed the joint
work in which they demonstrate this conception with the aid of
historical examples, *The German Ideology*, in the summer of
1846, Hess ' capitulated ' in the letter to Marx in which he recognizes the necessity of basing socialism ' on historical and
economic presuppositions ' instead of on ' ideology '—for the
time being only for propaganda purposes, but in the following
year we already see him attacking, in a language closely modelled
on that of Marx, the ' ideologist ' with his ' faith in ideas ', who
' abstracts from material conditions ', whilst a decade later
he still sees in ethics nothing more than ' a socio-economic
problem '.

Marx was not satisfied with Hess' accession to his views; on the
contrary it is precisely now that Marx rejects him emphatically [1]
and works up his rejection into a contemptuous attitude towards
him. But Hess' own soul was not satisfied either. It rebels against
the sacrifice of faith in the spirit and in nature to faith in society.
This rebellion is expressed fundamentally not in the sphere of the
social movement itself; though Hess afterwards departed again
from Marx and even quite openly supported Lassalle, there is
nothing to justify us regarding that as the stripping off of a
' disguise '. The rebellion of his soul does not move Hess to
attempt a new intellectual justification for socialism. He does not
retreat from the insight into the importance of material conditions for the development of social ends, but goes beyond it.
And in two ways. On the one hand, he is concerned to fit
socialism into a wider, supra-social, cosmic context, and not, as
Engels later attempted, following on from Haeckel (Marx himself pursued his own deep purpose in never concerning himself
with such ' metaphysics '), into a materialistically grounded context, but, following on from Spinoza, whom he had revered even
in his youth, into harmonious conformity to a law which
manifests itself in different spheres, the cosmic, the organic, the

[1] In the very year in which Hess professes his faith in them, Marx and Engels
declare with a gesture of superiority that they 'take no responsibility at all' for
Hess' writings.

psychical and the social, without any possibility of deriving one from the other. On the other hand, Hess attempts to mark off the social forces in the narrower sense from other forces which influence social developments, from a natural force, that of the 'race' and from an intellectual force, that of 'tradition'; race shapes social institutions into special types, tradition preserves the type and develops it. But whilst Hess proceeds perfectly objectively in his cosmological projects, here in the sphere of history his method is quite frankly subjective. He discovers the springs of the working of history in himself, in his nature, in his memory, in his connection with the generations which have produced him, with his own 'race' and with his own 'tradition'. And that is the very reason why he was blessed with really creative ideas in this sphere, in contrast to his cosmology, and at the same time, in contrast to his socialistic theories, with ideas which—for all the defects in their external composition—appear to us to form a uniform body of theory. By discovering the living spirit of Judaism in himself, he became aware of autonomous elements in the life of history which Marxism has either neglected or has only assimilated externally to this very day, without grasping their essential independence. In order to appreciate this fully we have merely to put in the place of the fluctuating concept of 'race' which Hess probably took over, though perhaps only indirectly, from Gobineau's *Essai*, that of national character, and in the place of the incomplete concept of 'tradition' that of creative faith—in doing which we do perfect justice to Hess' own intentions. In this way we gradually understand how it has come about that—whether he has been called a wrecked forerunner of Marx justly or unjustly—he is of decisive importance as the pioneer of the modern self-knowledge of the Jewish people.

Admittedly, it must still be noted that the discovery of Judaism was not something entirely new for Hess. In *Rome and Jerusalem* he took up again after a long period of time motifs which we find expressed in his very earliest writing, the *Sacred History of Humanity* of 1837. In this book he shows the Jews as the people, 'in whom the knowledge of God became hereditary', a statement that is not to be taken in a merely religious sense, on the contrary, in Judaism 'religion and politics, Church and State were intimately fused, had One Root, bore One Fruit. The Jews saw no difference between religious and political commandments, between duties towards God and duties towards Caesar. These and other antitheses cease to exist in view of a law which provided neither for the body nor the spirit alone but for both'. Certainly the Jews have not shown themselves worthy of this spiritual possession, the inherited knowledge of God. But now that the time is approaching in which the schism which arose in humanity after the downfall of the Jewish state is to be overcome, in which that original, since then so much disturbed unity is to be restored, 'religion and politics are to become one again'; now the Jews, this despised people, that has preserved its old customs so faithfully, has 'after a long sleep awakened again to a higher consciousness', this people is beginning 'to close its restless wanderings', in the Jews 'their old law is coming back to life', and this bears 'a more vital witness' to the holiness of this people 'than all the surviving documents of ancient times'. In Hess' second book, the *European Triarchy* of 1840, however, the hope fails to continue. True, 'Judaism must be finally regarded as the basic principle of the historic movement', and 'the Jews must be present as a spur in the body of western humanity, a kind of leaven'. True, 'the consciousness of the People of the Bible extends deepest into the past and into the future'. Nothing more is said, however, about the revival of the people as a people. The 'curse of rigidity' weighs down upon the children of Israel, since they have 'renounced their idea of the future'. They wander 'like a ghost across the living world, moved by the spirit of God', and can 'neither die, nor rise again', for 'the rejuvenating principle of Judaism, the Messianic belief, has ceased to exist'. During the time in which Hess is dependent on Marx, however, his original view of history changes into its very opposite. In the essay, *On the Nature of Money* of 1845, which was written under the spell of Marx's treatise, *On the Jewish Question*, which had appeared a year before, Hess—following Marx, who regards haggling as the 'secular cult of the Jews' and money as their 'secular God', and declares that he perceives an 'anti-social element' in Jewry, against which an 'emancipation of the human race from Jewry' should be initiated—can only report of the Jews that 'in the natural history of the social animals they had the world-historical task of working the beast of prey out of humanity', and 'and have now at last completed their professional task', since 'the mystery of Judaism and Christianity'

' has become manifest in the modern Jewish-Christian world of mercenary shopkeepers '. And after a further six years, in the French treatise, *Jugement dernier du vieux monde social*, the phrase about the ghost-like wanderings recurs with a strange intensification : the Jewish people, says Hess, has to ' wander like a ghost across the centuries—as a just punishment for its *spiritualistic* aberrations '. He has forgotten that on all its wanderings Jewry was never disloyal to that ' law, that provided neither for the body, nor for the spirit alone, but for both '. Ten years later, however, he writes *Rome and Jerusalem*. It is obvious that this represents a ' return ' in the early Jewish sense of the word. The motifs of the earlier work are taken up again on a higher level, and they now appear intimately personal and near at hand. Hess tells us that he drew the basic idea from the buried depths of his soul : ' For years this idea had been quivering buried alive in my locked-up breast, longing to escape.' Now he no longer intends merely to describe, but to confess.

What he confesses is first of all his ' twenty-year long [beginning about the time of the writing of the *European Triarchy*] alienation ' from Judaism and its ending, the new return to the ' midst of my people '—of the people that ' cannot coalesce organically with other nations '. He confesses that he had imagined that he had stifled the thought of his nationality in his breast for ever—note that he did not imagine that it had been stifled from without, but that he had stifled it himself (in the *European Triarchy* he had spoken of Jewish nationality as something for the lamentable continuance of which Christian legislation was to blame)—but that the idea had now proved itself a living one and had presented itself to him as a living idea. Now, however, he immediately takes a decisive step forward : this idea is inseparable from ' the holy land and the eternal city '. He considers the rediscovery of the people and the rediscovery of the land as ' inseparable '. But he regards this rediscovery as involving not merely an idea but also a decision : the decision ' to devote myself to the national rebirth of my people ', and this is necessarily at the same time the decision to devote himself to the rebuilding of the land. For ' Jewish patriotism ' is no mere intellectual formation, it is 'a true-to-nature feeling ', and that is why it is so closely connected with the memory of Palestine and the hope for Palestine.

Another train of thought leads to the same conclusion. National rebirth is impossible without the recovery of social health; in other words, without a return to a community life based on productive labour. The first condition for that, however, is ' a common native soil '. Without that man falls to the level of the ' parasite, who can only feed himself at the expense of foreign production.' This is already a recognition of the basic defect of the social structure of Jewry in exile and at the same time of the ' wide and free soil ' as the means of salvation, the soil that can be no other than the native soil in which the productive forces of the Jewish people are rooted and from which alone they can renew themselves.

A third train of thought is, however, still more important for Hess, one which, it is true, we first find adequately expressed in a treatise written in French soon after *Rome and Jerusalem*, as a supplement to that book, but which is probably the most important thing in all his thinking. Just as the first of these trains of thought is to be regarded as the presupposition of the second, so the second is to be regarded as the presupposition of the third. The true, the faithful Jews, Hess says, need *earth* ' to realize the historical ideal of our people, an ideal that is none other than the reign of God on *earth*.' In both cases, as in two earlier passages, Hess has underlined the word *la terre*, the earth. His first intention in thus emphasizing the word ' earth ' is to stress the fact the Jewish Messianic ideal refers not to the next world but to this : it is the earth that is to become the Kingdom of God ; but in order to fulfil its task of setting up the Kingdom of God the Jewish people needs ground under its feet, its own ground, a land on which it can build up an independent, self-determining life and therefore one in accordance with the will of God—for that it needs a land of its own. Hess here powerfully opposes the dissolution of the firm and simple Messianic faith into shadowy abstractions which was then dominant in Western Jewry, and his word remains true despite all later attempts of this kind. But at the same time and with no less force he thereby rejects all merely nationalistic, un-Messianic, anti-Messianic plans of restoring a Jewish Palestine as a state like other states, which deny the supranational task of the Jewish nation.

Hess' first book, the *Sacred History of Humanity*, was already strictly Messianic in its thought, but it contained no recognition

of the Messianic task of the Jewish people. Following the great
prophetic Christian of the twelfth century, Joachim de Fiore,
Hess saw the epoch of the Son following that of the Father and
that of the Holy Ghost following that of the Son. The latter had
begun intellectually with Spinoza and would find its social realization in the foundation of the ' new Jerusalem ', in which
' religion and politics would again be one ', a new Jerusalem,
furthermore, which would be set up ' in the heart of Europe '.
Thus at the beginning of the nineteenth century England's
prophetic poet, William Blake, had proclaimed the building of
Jerusalem ' in England's green and pleasant land ', and soon
after in the section ' To the Jews ' in his poem *Jerusalem* had
widened the announcement to cover the building of Jerusalem
' in every land '. The fact that in *Rome and Jerusalem* Hess now
assigns a special and fundamental task in the founding of the
Kingdom of God to a Jewish people resettling in Palestine does
not imply a weakening of his universalism but rather its deepening
by a return to the national universalism of the prophets of Israel.
Certainly ' Jerusalem ' is to be set up in the heart of Europe, but
the beginning of the enterprise must be the setting up of an
absolutely concrete Jewish Jerusalem; and this must be a real
Jerusalem, a Zion radiating its truth and righteousness across the
whole world.

Hess defines more closely the manner in which he sees the
' realization of the historical ideal of our people ' in Palestine : in
the creation of model social institutions. ' The first commandment
of God ', he says, ' that He has implanted in our hearts as the
creator of all the races, the source and basic principle of all the
others which have fallen to the lot of our people is that we are
ourselves to practise the law which we are commissioned to teach
the other historical peoples. The greatest punishment that has
been inflicted on us for deviating from the path traced out for
us by divine providence, that which has always oppressed our
people the most, is that, since we have lost the land (*la terre*),
we can no longer serve God as a nation through institutions
which cannot be continued and developed in our present exile,
since they presuppose a society founded in the land of our
ancestors. Yes, it is the land (*la terre*) that we lack, in order to
practise our religion.' Our religion, which means, in accordance
with Hess' fundamental conception, that religion which is in-

separably bound up with politics—no isolated sphere of worship
and theology, but the world of a faith the meaning and purpose
of which it is to be transformed into the living social activity of a
people. In *Rome and Jerusalem* and the supplementary treatises
Moses Hess comes forward as the first religious socialist in the
history of Judaism.

Hess speaks his mind even more clearly on the function which
will devolve on a Palestinian settlement in relation to the fulfilment of this task by the Jews. ' We too ', he writes in 1865 in
answer to a Christian author who had demanded a synthesis of
Hellas, Rome and Judea, ' believe in a revival of the genius of
our race, which only lacks a centre of activity around which a
nucleus of men devoted to Israel's religious mission could gather,
and from which there might then arise again the eternal principles which unite the human race with the universe and the
universe with its Creator. These men will find each other again
one day in the old community of Israel. Numbers are of no
importance in this matter. Judaism has never been represented
by a numerous people; the golden calf has always attracted the
greatest numbers, and a mere nucleus of Levites preserved the
holy flame of our religion burning on its ancient hearth.' The
concept of a centre is already an anticipation of the well-known
idea of Ahad-Ha'am, who refers to Pinsker but not to Hess and
who obviously was not acquainted with the latter's above quoted
French treatises. There is an important difference, however,
between Pinsker's concept of a ' national spiritual centre ' in
Palestine, as developed by Ahad-Ha'am, and Hess' concept of a
' centre of activity '. The former is concerned with cultural
creativity, the latter with social action; the former with the
reconstruction of the ' ruins of our spirit ' and the ' restoration to
our people of the honour of its name and its rightful place in the
temple of human civilization ', the latter with the renewal of the
great social ideas of Israel through the institutions of community
life. In the first case it is intended that the ' centre ' shall so
influence the ' periphery ', the diaspora, that ' the national spirit
will be renewed in all hearts ' and ' the feeling of national unity
strengthened in them ', it should ' purify the mind from the base-
ness of the Galut and fill the life of the spirit with a genuine
and natural spiritual content ', whereas in the second case the
task of the centre is to call on all those who have remained true

to Israel's basic and original task to rally round the great work
of realizing the ' eternal principles' in their own land and thereby
prepare the way for the fulfilment of the Messianic hope.
Ahad-Ha'am's eyes are fixed on the unity of the national spirit,
those of Hess, on the other hand, on ' the unity of theory and
life '. This unity, he says, ' can only be realized in its social
institutions by a nation which organizes itself politically '.

Even though Hess denies any fundamental importance to the
number of those taking part in the great work, nevertheless he
is certain that it can succeed only by the setting up of an independent community, by ' the restoration of the Jewish state '. He
merely counts on the majority of the people remaining where they
are as after the return from the exile in Babylon. The decisive
influence on the future of Judaism and its fulfilment of its duty
towards humanity, however, will be exerted by those who return
to Palestine and share in the great task.

In order to appreciate Hess' ideas aright, however, it must be
noted that Palestine appears to him in no sense as a land merely
handed on by tradition. He sees the future destiny of the Jewish
people in relation to the special geographical conditions of
Palestine and the world-wide economic importance which, thanks
to them, it is able to attain in our age. Palestine, ' the geographical centre of civilization ', lies ' on the future route to
India '. For Jewish settlements on this route there is ' no lack of
either Jewish workers or Jewish talents and capital '. These are
hints that we shall find again almost three decades later at the
beginning of the modern Zionist movement. But, unlike Herzl in
his first period, Hess by no means proposes a Jewish Palestine as a
' wall against Asia '; he expects it to reconcile ' modern Occiden-
tal culture with ancient Oriental culture '. It is especially
important, however, that Hess considers the possibilities resulting
from Palestine's geographical position in relation to the age-long
destiny that binds together this land and this people. He interprets
the reunion of the people and the land, to which he aspires, as the
ultimate fulfilment of an ancient divine plan : only this land
can develop from this people what it has within it, and, equally,
only this people can develop from this land what it has within it.

If Hess sees the share of a Jewish-Palestinian community in the
building up of a future humanity on such a large scale, he nevertheless pictures the beginnings of the work on a modest scale

and the development as organic. ' When,' he writes ' the world events which are shaping themselves in the Orient permit a practical start to be made with the restoration of the Jewish state, this beginning will probably consist first of all in the founding of Jewish colonies in the land of their ancestors.' ' And,' he says in another place, ' once a tiny seed has been planted under the protection of the great powers of Europe, the new tree of life will grow of its own accord and bear fruit.' The preconditions for this are, first, ' the acquisition of the national soil held in common ' —meaning the real common possession of the soil by the people ; secondly, ' the effort to establish legal conditions, under the protection of which the work can thrive '—the concept ' work ' is to be understood in its full social sense; and thirdly, ' the founding of Jewish societies for agriculture, industry, and commerce according to Mosaic, that is to say, socialistic principles ', a concise formulation which gives direct expression to Hess' religious socialism. ' These,' he continues, ' are the foundations on which Judaism will rise again in the Orient and by which the whole of Judaism will be revived.' Providing the full seriousness of each of the three points is grasped, there is little to add to them even today. Soon after the appearance of the book Hess stated his views on the language of the new community in a reply to Leopold Löw entitled *My Messianic Faith*. Leopold Löw had criticised the book. In this reply Hess stresses, as against the variety of Jewish dialects which was Löw's argument against the possibility of a national rebirth, the revival of the Hebrew language in our age.

This Open Letter shows most clearly the fusion of the religious and the socialistic in Hess' idea of Palestine. Löw had asked him in what the ' reformation of the whole social life ' to which he aspired would consist in a regenerated Jewish people. ' By what principles will it be guided? What ideal constitution will it have before it? The author is of course unable to answer that question.' Hess replies : ' Can it really have escaped your discerning mind that my whole book is a reply to this question? For what other reason have I turned to the Jewish people than because I have gained the conviction that this very people is called to be the first to realize these future institutions, the " Sabbath of history " which it was the first to proclaim?' And further : ' So long as this people had a common soil on which it was able freely to develop its spirit, on which it was able to realize it, it realized it in institutions and a literature which contain the guarantee of its consummation for the whole human race. Since the downfall of the Jewish state it was able to sanctify what it had created by means of religious observances which have a purely conservative character. There is no contradiction if I consider the spirit of the old Jewish institutions the basis of the institutions of the future and therefore want it to be preserved by religious observances which can only be based on the old institutions, and believe nevertheless that this very spirit will, once it is able to develop freely again on the soil of our forefathers, have the power to create new laws in accordance with the needs of the time and the people. The conservative religious observances of Judaism have only one meaning for us Jews, that of conserving our nationality for future creative functions. These will, like the old, again have a direct influence, as free productions of the Spirit, on the whole human race.'

On this most important subject, too, Hess does not remain on the level of pure ideas but advances towards its organic embodiment. A year after the letter to Löw, at the end of the last of his ten *Letters on Israel's Mission in Human History*, and obviously deliberately leaving it till the end, Hess explains how he conceives the first stages of the new constitutions. 'When the first Israelite pioneers', he says, 'take possession of our old fatherland and begin to cultivate it with the openly admitted purpose of laying the foundations for a political and social settlement', then the hour will also have come ' to elect a great Sanhedrin, in order to alter the law in accordance with the needs of the new society'. It almost seems as if we are further away from the fulfilment of this central task than the generation of the man who formulated it with such clarity.

Hess is the first to have expounded in the language of the contemporary world the ancient link between the Jewish people and Palestine and the task arising from it in our age. He was no 'forerunner', but an initiator, admittedly an initiator in thought and word, who died before the movement had even started. But even today, seventy-five years after his death, the Zionist movement has not yet really caught up with him.

THE PRESSING DEMAND OF THE HOUR
(*On Leo Pinsker and Theodore Herzl*)

OF THE two books from which the modern Zionist movement
proceeded, one is the *Auto-Emancipation* of Leo Pinsker, written
twenty years after Hess' *Rome and Jerusalem*, and the second,
Theodore Herzl's *The Jewish State*, which appeared fourteen
years later. Seen from the point of view of the history of ideas,
however, they both belong to an earlier stage than Hess' book,
in so far as it is permissible to regard the crisis of liberalism in
which they have their roots as 'earlier' than the rise of modern
socialism from which the former book emerged. With this is
connected the fact that both lack the objectively historical and
supra-historical foundations which we find in Hess. He—without
being aloof from the Jewish and general situation in which he
writes—is stirred by ancient and Messianic time, they by the
troubles and contradictions of the present hour. He speaks of
Israel's destiny, they speak of its relations with other peoples. In
other words : his mind is concentrated on action (the realization
of an equitable community life), theirs on reaction (emancipation
from anti-Semitism). The modern Zionist movement began with
a foreshortening of the idea. *Auto-Emancipation* is superior to
Hess' writings as far as diagnostic clarity and power of expression
are concerned ; *The Jewish State* is far superior to them as regards
the consistency and intellectual organization of the plan and its
technical construction, but the horizon of both of them is
narrower, or rather their vision does not penetrate to the point
where heaven and earth meet, in fact it does not even try to
reach that point, it does not receive the command to try. Despite
its political equipment the modern Zionist movement has been
given too little feeling for the world and world history during
its progress to maturity.

Pinsker, the doctor and rationalist of Odessa, born shortly
after 1820 and Herzl, the Viennese writer of feuilletons and
aesthete, born in 1860, ultimately represent the same type as far
as their historical function is concerned : the Jew startled out of
his liberalistic security. Pinsker was startled by the first pogroms,
Herzl chiefly by the Dreyfus affair. For both of them history is
the history of their own selves, in other words, fundamentally they

encountered the history of their own people in essentials only in
the shape of anti-Semitism, of the 'Other Side'; their own side
hardly became an intimate possession, hardly contributed to the
shaping of their lives. But more than that : both of them, cultured
men though they were, were hardly aware of history *as destiny*,
of the fateful power of history; for the very basis of liberalism is
to remain insensitive to the magnetism of history, however close
one's knowledge of it. Startled out of their sense of security, they
do not come to grips with history, with the meaning of insecurity,
but rather escape from it. They escape from it in order to secure
their community. It has rightly been pointed out that each of
them is treated as a neurasthenic when he communicates his
reactive plan to a friend : Pinsker, when he comes rushing to
the Rabbi Jellinek in Vienna, still unshaken out of his sense of
security, with the words : 'We want a fatherland, a homeland,
a small plot of earth on which we can live as human beings!';
Herzl, when he reads aloud to a fellow-journalist in a closed room
the speech he intends to address to the Rothschild family council
planned by him, which 'tells everything about the Promised
Land, except where it lies'. The contradiction contained in both
the utterances we have quoted is typical. A people or a section
of people can 'want' a land for immigration, a land to colonize,
but one cannot 'want' a 'fatherland', an indefinite fatherland.
Anyone who talks like that has been startled out of his sense
of security, but is not concerned with the restoration of a historical continuity but merely with a support to hold on to. The true
situation is even clearer in the case of Herzl. A 'promised' land
is essentially a quite definite land to which the giver of the
Promise points and not one of which it is still impossible to say
where it lies.'There is only one escape : into the Promised Land!'
Herzl wrote two weeks before in notes for a conversation with
Baron Hirsch. 'It exists. We can create it for ourselves. We are
going to build a new world for ourselves (I don't know : perhaps
in the Argentine).' That is the style of a feuilleton writer,—a
style suitable for making a momentary impression in the moment
of reading (feuilleter = turning over the leaves), but not for with-
standing the scrutiny of a later thinker. Naturally one can
'create' and 'build' settlements and if one likes, one can also,
as Christian settlers in America and elsewhere have done, give
them Biblical names; but the term 'Promised Land' deserves

to be treated carefully by a people to whom a land, a quite definite land, was once 'promised'. 'Promised Land' implies a belief in a power that promises and gives; and the strength of such a faith cannot be replaced by even the most enthusiastic planning. Herzl reports in his Diary that the colleague to whom he read aloud the speech to the Rothschilds said to him: 'Someone tried to do that in the last century [the little historical blunder 'in the last' instead of 'in the seventeenth' has its place in the picture]: Sabbatai!' It was then that Herzl apparently heard for the first time of the pseudo-Messianic figure around whom the most passionate Palestine movement of the Diaspora broke out and with whom he has later—wrongly—often been compared. The Diary continues: 'Yes, in the last century it was not possible. Now it is possible—because we have machines'. Herzl's veneration for the age of technical achievement, in which he saw a 'delightful Renaissance', finds its strongest expression here. But just as the collapse of that Messianic movement did not come from the lack of machines, so, useful as they are, not machines but the power of authentic faith will decide the ultimate success of the Zionist work of settlement.

'The Promised Land', Herzl says in another entry a day before the reading,' is there whither we take it!' Considered from a literary or oratorical point of view that is a beautifully pointed statement, but it is not true. Herzl substantiates it by saying that everyone takes ' a piece of the Promised Land in himself and with himself into the land itself. The one in his head, another in his hands and a third in his savings.' So the 'Promised Land' is even alleged to reside in a man's purse! By such a far-reaching 'secularization' of the religious vocabulary it is not merely transferred to a foreign world but it is deprived of the very sap of its life. Whether within the religious tradition or outside it, it is of crucial importance to know that what is planned for the people and the land stems not from reflection but from a destiny embedded in the origins of time. To be sure, it is important to decide and act oneself, but in the last analysis it all depends on whether one decides and acts as one who is carrying out a mission.

If we consider the development of the two men as Zionists we shall be in a better position to realize the nature of the question presented to the modern Zionist movement from its beginnings.

Pinsker introduced the words spoken to Jellinek into his treatise

in somewhat modified terms. Here he says, ' that we are nowhere
at home, and that at last we must have a home, if not a fatherland of our own '. Under certain circumstances, we are told here,
one must forgo a ' fatherland '; a ' homeland ', however, is the
indispensable factor. This stress on the forgoing of a fatherland
can obviously only mean that one must be ready to renounce
one's connection with one's forefathers in choosing a homeland,
that it is possible to possess a home, a feeling of home and homely
security without this connection. In his Hebrew translation of the
Auto-Emancipation, Ahad-Ha'am rendered the words ' a homeland ' by ' some place reserved for us '; this is incorrect, for all
the associations bound up with the word ' homeland ' are lost
in this rendering. Pinsker really means a land, which one comes
to regard as home, in which one feels at home. That can happen
in other places beside the fatherland. The most important thing,
Pinsker writes in a letter after the appearance of the *Auto-
Emancipation*, is that the Jews should use all their forces ' to
create something similar to a fatherland of our own '.

Shortly before that passage in his book, it is true, he reproaches
the Jews for having forgotten their fatherland in the course of
the generations as well as for being without a fatherland. ' Is
it not really time ', he asks, ' to realize how disgraceful this is for
us ?' But he does not conclude from that that the connection with
the fatherland should be remembered; what is needed is ' a safe
homeland ', ' a new and suitable dwelling '. And Pinsker goes
beyond this. He speaks of the unorganized and most unsuccessful
attempts at settlement from the period which directly followed
the pogroms. ' The national consciousness ', he says, ' exploded
before our eyes in the mass of the Russian and Rumanian Jews
in the form of an irresistible urge to go to Palestine. Wrong as
this urge turned out to be judging by the results, nevertheless it
bears witness to the right instincts of the people who now realize
that they need a home.' An ' irresistible urge ' to go to Palestine
manifests itself among the people, but for Pinsker that is no proof
that the people feels an urge to go *to Palestine*, but merely that it
has become clear ' that it needs *a home* '. The highly intelligent
and high-minded man has not the slightest idea of how contradictory the two sentences are which he wrote down there one
after the other. For him the word ' Palestine ' obviously suggests
a retrogression, a retreat from Western civilization.

In these circumstances it is hardly surprising that he pronounces himself directly opposed to a fundamental decision in favour of Palestine. ' If we are anxious to secure a home for ourselves,' he says, ' then above all we must not dream of restoring the old Judea. ' This " above all " should be noted : the very first essential is that a clean sweep should be made with such romantic ideas ! And he goes on : ' The goal of our efforts should now be not the " holy " land, but a land " of our own ".' The point of these remarks is obviously aimed at orthodoxy as a factor of reaction but, with the abuse of the Holy, the Holy itself is attacked. And again he continues : ' We want to take there the most sacred things we have saved from the shipwreck of what was once our fatherland : the idea of God and the Bible. For it is only these and not Jerusalem or the Jordan that have made our fatherland the Holy Land.' As so often, the ' idea of God ' stands in the way of the living God and the Bible as a total possession in the way of what is said in the Bible. It goes without saying that Palestine did not make itself the Holy Land, but what made it the Holy Land was its election by the living God and His promise, of which the Bible is the record. What is the point of the Jews taking somewhere or other an idea of God which they have sterilized by their departure from the action of God and a Bible which they have deprived of its content, as ' their most sacred ' possession ? A ' most sacred ' possession is always tied to memory and hope, to places and events, to this-and-not-that, here-and-nowhere-else. But Pinsker now continues : ' Possibly the Holy Land could also become our own land. In that case all the better . . .' This ' all the better ' sounds rather strange after what has gone before. But, thank heavens, things do not happen like that in the reality of history : one does not choose the most expedient and attainable among various possibilities, but one goes straight for the goal of one's desire and stakes one's life to reach it.

' It lies in the very nature of our task ', says Pinsker, ' that we have a unique asylum to counterbalance our dispersal '. But what is supposed to guarantee the uniqueness of this asylum if there is no objective connection between the people and the land ? Pinsker sees ' the death germ for the whole movement ' in the schism that arose in his day between the tendency to migrate to Palestine on the one hand and to the Argentine on the other. But how can repeatedly new schisms be avoided if the voice of expediency is always to be followed? Indeed, when one hears Pinsker talking thus of 'those two countries situated in opposite parts of the world', 'which have been recently contesting each other's right to precedence', and remembers that one of them is Erets-Israel and the other a territory that is alleged to come into question for quite accidental reasons, then one sees immediately before one the 'death germ', which assumed the name of Uganda in Herzl's time and after him that of territorialism.

'Far, very far distant,' Pinsker cries, 'is the harbour we are seeking with our souls. At the moment we do not even know whether it is in the East or the West. But no journey can be too long for the wanderer across a thousand years.' Pinsker does not detect the irony that lies in the quotation he uses. It is no indefinite land, simply corresponding to the need of the moment, that Goethe's Iphigenia 'seeks with her soul', but the land of the Greeks, the unique and irreplaceable land. And if the wanderer through a thousand years still does not know where he is wandering to, then no comparison of his chances of success in Palestine and the Argentine can make him any the wiser. 'We sailed', Pinsker cries, 'without a compass on the turbulent ocean of world history, and it is up to us to make one.' This image is also not a particularly fortunate one: it is a well-known fact that the magnetic needle constantly points in *one* direction and is therefore more suitable as a simile for the faithful love of Zion than for the territorialism which is still looking for a goal.

'The *age-old* idea that I have thrown into Jewry . . .', Pinsker writes in a letter soon after the appearance of the *Auto-Emancipation*. But the age-old idea that he means is that of the exclusiveness of Zion and not that of the acquisition of a special territory of which it is not yet known for a certainty where it is, which is expressed in his book.

When Pinsker's idea—in contrast to the opposition which he met in the West—was received with enthusiasm in the circles of the friends of Zion in Eastern Europe, he allowed himself to be persuaded by them to give Palestine preference as the idea goal of the masses of the people, but he refused to make this preference a matter of principle. If we collate Pinsker's speech at the opening of the Kattovitz Conference—the first attempt to centralize the modern Zionist movement—of 6 November 1884 with his public and epistolary utterances of approximately the same period, his modified view of the matter turns out to be: 1. In principle a congress of world Jewry should decide on the choice of the land (this decision is part of what is called 'the national resolution' in the *Auto-Emancipation*). 2. But as the Jews of the West take a negative attitude and a part of Eastern Jewry is indifferent, the remainder, in other words the section of the people prepared to take action, must stand for the whole and its will must be taken as representing the decision of the people. 3. This will or, as Pinsker repeatedly terms it, 'the instincts of the people', which 'does not err' because the section of the people ready to take action is in fact the real people and only what the real people wants can be realized for the people, tends unmistakably towards Palestine. Pinsker adds that he rejoices at this decision of the people. This is a recurrence on a higher level of the old phrase 'all the better'. But one would be wrong to assume that Pinsker had thereby abandoned the standpoint of expediency and had recognized something of the objective connection between the people and the land. It must not be forgotten that he had already found the 'instinct of the people' 'correct' in the *Auto-Emancipation* because the people had realized that 'it needs a home'; even now he has come no further than that. Therefore he refuses to rephrase the alternative expressed in that book into a fundamental decision for Palestine: he chooses the settlement of Palestine because it is realizable, and it is realizable because the people wants it, and the people wants it—yes, that is the question, why? Simply because it wants a home. And because it wants a home its choice of a home is right,—it is impossible to discover any other argument in Pinsker. Beyond that there remains only his feeling of rejoicing at the decision of the people. In other words, he discovered a feeling for Palestine in himself which he shares with the people; but where this feeling comes from, whether it is merely a product of tradition or the expression of an objective relationship—he does not touch this central question and he evidently regards it as non-existent. 'If previously we were', Pinsker says in his opening speech at the Kattovitz Conference, 'the vehicles of the traffic between man and man, we are now returning to mother nature who gratefully blesses the hands that cultivate her and knows no other difference among men but that of the spirit.' In the translation of the speech contained in

the Hebrew minutes of the meeting the following takes the place
of the second part of this sentence : ' Let us now return to our
old mother the land that waits for us in great mercy, waits to
feed us with its fruits and satisfy us with its goodness.' This
certainly expresses the feelings of the lovers of Zion and that of
Pinsker as one of them, but it is not what Pinsker said as an
initiator and leader, nor is it what he thought as the designer of
his plan.

After a series of serious disappointments both in modest
attempts at settlement and in organization—he had already fore-
seen the essentials of this ' fight for the honour of our noble but
deeply degenerate people, with our own degenerate brothers as
opponents ' after the publication of the *Auto-Emancipation* and
yet was bitterly disappointed when it came to it—Pinsker
expressed himself in conversation as having resigned himself to
the fact that Palestine was not fitted to offer a safe asylum, but
he thought that its settlement should be promoted and extended
as far as possible ; ' we can and should found a spiritual national
centre in Palestine '. This utterance has come down to us in an
essay by Ahad-Ha'am who was one of the audience and his own
idea of a 'spiritual centre' has been traced back to it. But
Pinsker's statement and Ahad-Ha'am's teaching differ precisely
on the most essential point of all. The basis of the former is
obviously the opinion that another place must be sought for the
necessary national asylum; Ahad-Ha'am knows no such parallel
tendency and activity. Accordingly, the word 'spiritual'
obviously has a limiting connotation in Pinsker—not the asylum
that saves the people, but merely a centre of its spiritual life—
whereas it has no such meaning in Ahad-Ha'am : his centre signifies the *unique* gathering together of the combined national
strength of the people and therefore it is not, as with Pinsker,
merely spiritual; 'spiritual' here means that its active relation
to the periphery can only be an inward, moral, and cultural, not
a political, one.

The factor of personal development is far more forcibly
stressed in Herzl, which is naturally to be explained not merely
by the difference of temperament but also by that of age.

As for Pinsker, so for Herzl too it is, to begin with, merely a
question of expediency, which land is to be chosen. During the
time in which the treatise on the ' Jewish state ' was taking shape

he weighs the arguments for and against Palestine again and again. The arguments for are that it ' was the unforgotten ancestral seat of our people ', that ' the name alone would be a programme in itself ', and that 'it would exert a strong attraction on the masses '—in a word : ' the mighty legend '. Against : first, that most of the Jews are no longer Orientals and have grown accustomed to quite different climates ; secondly, that a settlement in Palestine could not expand sufficiently ; thirdly, ' Europe is too near, and in the first quarter of a century of our existence we must have, for our enterprise to thrive, peace from Europe and from its military and social entanglements'. Which means that propaganda reasons are an argument for Palestine—it is easier to arose a mass movement with this catchword; the arguments against it lie in the cause itself—it is not entirely suitable as a land for settlement.

' Fundamentally ' Herzl was at that time—so he intends to put it to the Rothschilds—' neither against Palestine nor for the Argentine'; but it is clear from the distribution of the words ' against' and ' for ' in this sentence that he tended more towards America at this time. And when, shortly before in the same draft, we read : ' I thought for a time of Palestine ', that can only be taken as meaning that it was at least not in the forefront of his thoughts at the moment of writing. It is true that, shortly before, he specifies 'negotiations with *Zion* ' as one of the first tasks, but he is obviously merely referring here to discussions with the already existing Zionists to win them over to the new movement.

Eight months after these diary entries, *The Jewish State* appears. Here the balance is restored, only the Argentine is spoken of in the manner of a business-like calculation of the prospects, whilst Palestine is referred to with a solemn emphasis on its emotional value. ' Palestine is our unforgettable historical homeland. This name alone would be a powerfully moving rallying-cry for our people.' As a result of changing moods Palestine has now come more decidedly into the foreground (we do not know to what influences this is to be attributed), but the distribution of the motifs has remained the same. The points mentioned in favour of the Argentine are its wealth, its area, its sparse population, its moderate climate ; while the only factor mentioned in favour of Palestine is its emotional value, which means, in this context, its value for mass propaganda. The question as to

Palestine's objective qualification is not raised, let alone the
question as to the relationship between the people and the land
which was the basis of and which preserves its emotional value.

The publication of his first statements about his plan and then
that of the book itself brought Herzl into touch with the Lovers
of Zion movement, in other words, with the concrete trend to
Palestine. The fact that groups and personalities everywhere en-
thusiastically regarded his plan as the deed which is needed to give
the idea political substance and to secure the political framework,
made a powerful impression on him. At the same time, however,
the reactions among Eastern and Western Jewry were consider-
ably different. That of the East corroborated his view of the propaganda value of the name of Palestine; that of the West, on the
other hand, introduced a new factor, it enlightened him as to the
peculiar suitability of Palestine. Already before the appearance
of the book, his visit to London, where he expounded his plan
to a larger circle for the first time, had influenced him in this
direction. Here he heard from qualified people that Palestine had
'a great hinterland', that it was possible to think of a 'greater
Palestine', and at the same time that the Argentine was unfavourable and 'that only Palestine could possibly come into the
question', that 'England's pious Christians would help, if we
were to go to Palestine', and so on; Herzl 'suddenly finds himself in a different world'. He also heard a number of positive
views on the prospects from prominent English Jews, as for
example when old Sir Samuel Montagu stated that 'one might
offer the Sultan two million pounds for Palestine'; this figure of
two millions recurs later on in the history of the Zionist movement, first in the negotiations with Constantinople and then as
the share capital of the Jewish Colonial Bank. All this strongly
influenced Herzl in favour of Palestine; particularly as it came
from England, a country that had impressed him from his youth
upwards. It is true that he evidently made no further alterations
in this direction in the book that was already completed to all
intents and purposes at the time of the London journey, but the
influence of the English atmosphere was a lasting one. After the
appearance of the 'Jewish State' there is no longer any mention
of the choice of land as still having to be made; the decision
that is treated in the first book as a problem of the future that
will have to be settled after a scrupulous examination of all the

circumstances, has already been taken when the ' Jewish State
appears.

The reasons, however, which Herzl now quotes *vis-à-vis* the
public and presumably also *vis-à-vis* himself, in favour of Palestine, have hardly changed. In essentials it is still the old theme :
the emotional value that the land has for the Jewish masses. Only
the formulation has gained in concreteness. ' What Baron Hirsch
failed to achieve in Argentine,' Herzl says in the first of his
polemical articles, more than a year after the appearance of the
Jewish State, ' is succeeding in Palestine. Why? Because " national
Judaism " is fertilizing the old soil. . . . A land, capable of rearing
all cultures, with long dormant mineral wealth and yet worth
nothing to others because others are unable to lead to it the
fertilizing streams of men obedient to Zionism.' Admittedly, it
still remains obscure here whether in his opinion they would have
still obeyed it if the decision to build a Zion in the Argentine had
been reached; it is still not clear whether Herzl means at rock
bottom the emotional relationship of the people to Palestine or
the national-political character of his plan. He expresses this
more precisely later on in a polemical speech, a year after the
appearance of the *Jewish State*, ' We think,' he says, 'that this
land is particularly suitable because we still continue to be
related to it by an ideal tie.' But on what reality is the ideality of
this tie founded? On a tradition, on a memory, or on something more, on a historically objective relationship that is as real
today as ever? Only once, once again six months later, in the
opening speech at the second Zionist Congress, does Herzl go a
step further. ' Admittedly, the building site that is suitable for
us,' he says, ' is one of a special kind. . . . Ideas for the whole of
humanity have grown on this soil on which now so little grows.
And that is the very reason why no one will be able to deny that
there is an evergreen relationship between our people and this
land.' The claim of the people of Israel to the land of Israel rests
therefore on the productivity of their first encounter. Only one
further step was needed and Herzl would have confronted the
historical and supra-historical problem of this productivity, the
problem of its origin and therefore at the same time the problem
of a destiny. Herzl did not take this further step and probably he
could not take it.

We read at the end of the Congress speech : ' We are striving

for our old land.' But eight weeks before this Herzl wrote in
his diary: ' I am thinking of giving the movement a territorial
aim, keeping Zion as the ultimate goal. The poor masses need
immediate help and Turkey is not yet so lost that she would
consider our wishes. . . . They still say that they would not think
of giving us Palestine. Therefore we must organize ourselves for
an immediately attainable goal under the flag of Zion, maintain-
ing all our historical claims. We can perhaps demand Cyprus
from England and even consider South Africa or America—
until the dissolution of Turkey. *C'est encore à creuser pro-
fondément.* I must discuss it with Nordau before the Congress.'
It is clear from the final words that Herzl considered whether
he should not make a communication in the direction indicated
to the Congress, possibly in the opening address. This did not
happen and in the immediately following years he probably
still thought of Cyprus as a spring-board to Palestine but
apparently neither of America nor South Africa as a land suitable for settlement. The fact, however, that he mentioned them
in that diary entry is important for an appreciation of Herzl's
inner approach to the subject as also of his later attitude to the
Uganda project. His constant concern is the early execution of
his plans for a settlement as an answer to the need of the
masses and to the ' Jewish problem ' in all its oppressive urgency;
this ' refuge ' must be created as quickly as possible wherever it
can be created. After the writing of the ' Jewish State ' this
dominating impulse remained unchanged. But Herzl can and
will not now carry out his plan other than ' under the flag of
Zion'. He can do no other, for the popular movement which
he leads is based on the idea of Zion and would lose its unity
and power without it, but he does not wish to either since the
symbol of 'Zion' has overwhelmed his heart and his own cause
is henceforth inseparable from it. Without really knowing either
of them he has entered into a covenant not merely with the
masses but also with the depths of history, a covenant that is
indissoluble. The relationship between people and land with
which he does not occupy himself influences him. In the immediately succeeding years he refers again to the ' ideal
factor' (1899) that speaks in favour of Palestine and to its
' ideal power of attraction for the masses ' (1900). Consciously
he gets no further than the ideality of Palestine. But the hidden

reality which is merely mirrored in this ideality communicates itself to him without his knowledge.

The power of the symbol—not of the propagandistically usable pseudo-symbol of our day, but of the authentic symbol which is a material representation of a hidden reality—on Herzl's mind is most clearly apparent in the 'novel with a purpose', *Old-New Land*, which he wrote between 1899 and 1902. As a novel the book is worthless, but it is an important document of a person and a cause—indeed, of the intimate relation between a person and a cause. In the period in which the plan of a Jewish state was arising Herzl had already considered the idea of putting it in the form of a novel, which was to be called *The Promised Land* (one must remember the arbitrariness with which he was treating the concept at the time); and in a strange way the political plan and utopian literature, the sphere of action and the sphere of fiction alternate. 'In the notes,' he remarks himself in the Diary on the preceding entries, 'the Jewish State is sometimes thought of as a reality, sometimes as the material for a novel.' At times, it seems a 'puzzle' to him how he 'came from the ideas of the novel to the practical ideas'; that is, when he firmly believes in the realization of his plan. But whenever the fear that he will not be taken seriously predominates, he again turns deliberately to literature; 'now', he writes, ' I am thinking seriously again of the novel, because everyone will probably regard my plan as a phantasy'. This up and down movement, so characteristic of a man who, though lacking real poetic gifts, had a great and effective imagination, is repeated some years later when he is working at *Old-New Land*. According as to whether the prospects of realizing the plan were favourable or unfavourable and according to the state of his ideas concerning them he either turns to or away from work on the novel. If ' the categorical No ' were to come from Constantinople (he enters this too in his diary), he would go on writing the novel, ' for then our plan would be a mere novel and belong solèly to the future '. For him anything that stands no chance of being realized in the *present* is a novel. If the prospects improve, then he leaves the novel on one side again, the novel ' that becomes increasingly bad and dull the longer it stands '. But at the end we read : ' The hopes of success in the practical sphere have faded, my life is no novel now. So the

novel is my life.' What he really needs is that his life should be
' a novel'; writing novels is only a substitute for that. (In the
same way he had once felt that he was a ' dramatist' when he
was planning the speech to the family council of the Rothschilds). Less than seven weeks after that, *Old-New Land* is
finished. The fact that writing the novel was a substitute had an
unfavourable influence on the literary value of the book; but its
great documentary value comes from Herzl's having thrown
into it everything he wanted to realize and was not allowed to
realize. *Old-New Land* has been not unfairly criticized for not
having a national cultural content. Herzl was in fact concerned
from the very beginning not with national particularities but
with universal international humanity, though he admittedly
did not appreciate adequately that a new humanity capable of
standing up to the problems of our time can come only from the
co-operation of national particularities, not from their being
levelled out of existence. He did not recognize this sufficiently;
nevertheless the humanity that speaks out of the book is not a
shallow and abstract humanity but that of the common struggle
of all peoples for the true life. The community described in the
book is called ' the new society'; in the letter with which he
sends it to the Grand Duke of Baden he says: ' The book deals
with the question of a new society. I believe that all the nations
are always on the road to a new society.' That is not an anational
claim but a national-humanistic one and perhaps of all that
Herzl wrote it comes nearest to the legacy of the prophets of
Israel. But the national element was not so foreign to
him either as it appears to be. A remarkable diary entry
of March 1898 on the never executed plan for a three-
volume novel bears witness to that; in it Herzl intended to tell
how a Viennese Jewish journalist founds a thoroughly honest
daily newspaper with a German nationalist bias, how the
enterprise collapses after some initial success and the hero leaves
Vienna in disgrace; ' but he had discovered Zion', and he em-
barks for Palestine. On this Herzl observes: ' In the first volume
the hero hears of a small crazy band of neo-Hebrews (Smolenski,
Bierer) who seem to him like strange Asiatics. From time to time
a note from the silently growing band emerges until at the close
of the novel their joyful song of victory bursts forth in a great
chord.' This unrealized possibility must not be overlooked if

one wants to obtain a just picture of the extraordinary man and
his world of ideas. But there is also something in the texture of
Old-New Land that witnesses to a deeper relationship between
Herzl and Judaism; it is precisely that of which I said that it
shows the power of the symbol over his mind. I mean the
passage in which a speech against those trends towards ' assimilation ' is reported which had degraded Zion to a concept without
concrete geographical foundation, in fact to a mere phrase which
demanded that ' Zion should be understood as meaning something
different from Zion—anything except the one true Zion '.
But in the same speech the people is warned against leaving the
ground on which the ' new society ' is to be founded, the ground
of human love. Zion is only Zion when this ground is preserved. In the first part of the speech the concrete geographical
Zion had been defended against every kind of spiritualistic
evaporation of the concept; but here, at the end, the vital
additional point is made that this concrete geographical Zion is
only then truly Zion if it realizes the prophetic meaning which
once filled out the name, if, therefore, its new construction is
built on the foundation of human love. This is the pure unfolding of Herzl's national humanism. All nations are always on
the way to a new society; but within what is common to all
nations there is a particular Jewish type of society which has
a special importance for the development of a real humanity;
it is this characteristically Jewish type of society that is called
Zion. This name, the fullness of whose meaning has grown to
maturity through many generations of Jewish national history,
is the expression of the specific relationship between this people
and this land. The real ' lovers of Zion ' and the real ' Zionists '
believe in the validity of this relationship. It is only from this
point of view that the innermost purpose of the novel *Old-New
Land* is to be understood.

But, as we have said already, this novel was completed because
' the hopes of success in the practical sphere had faded ', or
rather because they seemed to have faded to Herzl, for whom,
it must be remembered, ' success ' was identical with political
success, with the creation of political ' conditions ' before the
creation of colonizational ' deeds '. The incongruity between the
prospects of success in this sense and the pressing needs of the
Jewish people becomes more apparent to Herzl than ever. It is

not a diplomatic phrase, but the expression of his real feeling
that he expresses to Joseph Chamberlain shortly after the
appearance of *Old-New Land*, whom he tells in circumspect
terms of the standstill in the Constantinople negotiations, in
order to ask him for Cyprus and the Sinai peninsula : ' Now I
have time to negotiate, but my people has not. They are starving
in the pale. I must bring them immediate help.' He *must* help, *he*.
It was the need of the Jewish people that had called him in the
first place and in the seven years its call has become louder, not
softer. What is Zion if it does not exist for their sake? He,
Theodore Herzl, must get down to his real work—certainly too
because only it can redeem him from the fictitious world of his
literary activity, but still more because he can thereby redeem
the Jews from the sufferings which he knows so intimately from
the inside, which he felt so deeply in the days when he was a
student among German students. He may also have had a pre-
sentiment that henceforward no long span of life was to be
allotted to him : ' man's life is short ', he says later on to
Chamberlain. At any rate, he now knows that he is under a
compulsion to act. There can and there must be no contradiction between this ' compulsion ' and ' Zion '. Since his diary
entry : ' I am thinking of giving the movement a more immediate
territorial goal, keeping Zion as the ultimate aim ', he has
waited for four years with his eye on the changing chances in
Constantinople (in fact they did not change, no one there supported his programme at all, they were merely playing with
him); now the matter has become deadly serious. In September
1902, before the interview with Chamberlain, he still refuses to
consider the possibility of South Africa; in April 1903, in the
second conversation with the Minister, when the latter refers
him to Uganda and says : ' It has occurred to me that that would
be a land for Dr Herzl, but he only wants to go to Palestine
or somewhere near it, for some sentimental reason or other ', he
still replies : ' Yes, I *must* ' (from this side too the *I must* recurs),
and continues : ' We must have the basis in or near Palestine.
Later we can also colonize Uganda ', But a month afterwards,
when the prospect of Cyprus vanishes and there are reports that
the prospect of Al'Arish is vanishing too, he shows himself inclined to agree to an East African proposal, for the ' state of
distress in which our people finds itself impels us to take speedy
and large-scale action '. And just as every step that he has taken

receives the consecration of a fundamental decision and every decision is founded on a plan, though the plan may come after the decision has already been taken, so now, in order to confirm his attitude to Zion and his own feeling for Zion he works out ideas on a strangely broad basis. The new system is most precisely expounded in letters to Max Nordau of July 1903. 'We must,' Herzl writes, 'make the politics of this hour.' It is the hour of Kishinev. The news of the pogrom—'the lamentable events of Kishinev', as they are called in a letter from Herzl to Plehve written at the time the Uganda offer was being made—stirred up the Jews all over the world. Herzl hears the first minutes of this hour as they strike: it is only the beginning. 'Kishinev is not finished', he wrote to Lord Rothschild, and now he writes to Nordau: 'We must give an answer to Kishinev and this is the only possible one.' *We must*—here the *must* recurs again in the most up-to-date guise possible. But 'this', the only answer, in other words the only possible answer is to begin the Jewish state by founding daughter settlements 'elsewhere'. In other words: 'an inverted England *in parvo*', or: 'the inverted building of an England in the waistcoat-pocket.' The first of these colonies, on which the motherland is to be built, might be in East Africa; but such 'nests and power stations of Zionism' are to be set up in other parts of the world as well; thus 'a charter in Argentine might result in a second power station'. Morocco and other areas are also contemplated. The spatial distance of the power stations from one another is irrelevant; it is immaterial where a start is made. 'It is a question of opportunity where we drive in the first stakes into the lagoon, provided we are clear about what house to set on the foundation. This is the State of the Jews. That was and is what I am out for. It would naturally be marvellous to start with Erets Israel. But if that will not work then a beginning must be made somewhere else.' Erets Israel, Herzl says, would be marvellous 'to start with'. The 'Jewish state' now means for him Palestine together with a number of colonies all over the world; if the building of this complicated structure cannot be begun at the centre, then it must begin somewhere on the periphery. This encircling of Palestine with an extensive ring of Jewish land set up 'on a national basis', until it will be possible to advance to Palestine itself from these outposts, is 'the new way of Zionism'. A clean sweep must be made with the ingrained idea that the foundations of the building can only be laid in Palestine, for 'we are the makers of formulas but not their prisoners'. 'This British East African beginning is *politically* a Rishon-le-Zion,[1] certainly nearer to Zion than what Baron Edmund Rothschild set up.' 'Conditions' elsewhere, however far the place is from Palestine and fundamentally foreign to it though it be as Uganda, are more than 'deeds' in Palestine. With this Herzl's overestimation of political action as opposed to colonization is pushed to its extreme limit, his lack of understanding of the great historical fact that the essential function of politics is not to change conditions but to register and sanction changes that have taken place. This merely political perspective, certainly contrary to Herzl's will, causes the living symbol of Zion, the symbol of whose power he had had personal experience, the symbol which is the material representation of the hidden reality, to evaporate into the politico-propagandistic sham symbol of our day. The 'new way' proceeds from a political myth. The daringly imaginative Theodore Herzl thinks and says : 'This way will lead to Zion '; but the underlying reality, that is, the reality that would have become ascendant if the Uganda plan or a similar plan had been realized, is that people would behave as if this way led to Zion. 'Our immediate programme of relief', Herzl writes to Nordau, 'is the publicly and legally reorganized settlement possibly elsewhere, but naturally holding the flag of Zion high, in fact higher than ever, the flag under which we are gathering ourselves and our forces.' Herzl says and means : 'the flag of Zion ', but the reality which would be covered by this flag would no longer be that of Zion, but that of the Jewish State. And Herzl is by no means lacking in awareness of the change that he is bringing about or wants to bring about—only he sees this change simply as a return to his original plan for a Jewish state and this return simply as the annulment of the plan modification performed by the Zionist programme. 'With that ', he writes to Nordau, 'we still or once more stand by the programme for a Jewish State, that we weakened a little for Palestine for opportunistic reasons.' But he does not see that the putting into effect of this change would necessarily mean the surrender of that innermost reality of national history and

---

[1] Rishon-le-Zion, i.e., First for Zion (Isaiah 41, 2f) is the name of a settlement founded in 1882 by the Baron Edmund Rothschild.

national destiny to which the name of Zion refers. When, at the end of the Uganda Congress, he repeats the Psalmist's vow, 'If I forget thee, oh Jerusalem', with raised hand, as a binding oath, it is certainly no empty gesture of appeasement but the expression of the truth of his heart; but after the final session of the Congress he admits to his friends: 'The rift goes right through the centre of my person.' In the 'Letter to the Jewish People' which he drafts ten weeks later, he puts it even more precisely. 'The path is dividing,' the letter begins, 'and the division cleaves the leader's breast.' And further on in the same letter we read: 'If it comes to a schism, my heart will remain with the Zionists and my mind with the Africans. This is the kind of conflict that I can only solve by my resignation.' But the division which cleft his breast was certainly not so simple as he sees it here. His heart was also with the sufferings of the Jews and therefore in the East Africa project as the nearest-to-hand attempt to overcome them, and at the same time his mind was in the cause of Zion which brought him into touch with the dream of the masses and thereby gave him his power over them. In the above-mentioned conversation with his friends after the Sixth Congress he tells them that 'if he lives to see it', he will say at the seventh Congress: 'Although originally merely a supporter of the idea of the Jewish state—*n'importe où*—I have nevertheless later seized the flag of Zion, and I have myself become a Lover of Zion.' And he also repeats this in the 'Letter to the Jewish People': 'When I started out I was only a Jewish State supporter, I have become a Lover of Zion.' He does not say a 'Zionist', which like all 'isms' merely implies an opinion, but 'Chovev Zion', Lover of Zion, and love is no mere opinion but a feeling and more than that. One senses from the way he repeats the statement how deeply the fact that he loves occupies him in the depths of his soul, how it astonishes and moves him and how he cherishes it with care. In very fact he did become, like Pinsker, a Lover of Zion through his contact with the common people. But like Pinsker he does not penetrate as far as Zion itself with this love, does not reach the historical and supra-historical mystery that this name implies. Whosoever attains thus far, in his breast there is no longer any division.

'If I live to see it', Herzl says at the end of August to his friends about the next Congress. He did not live to see it. 'I myself am constantly very unwell ', he writes two weeks later to a doctor friend. ' Cardiac neurosis! That and the Jews will be my death.' By 'the Jews' he certainly means in this context primarily the passionate and reckless opposition which had fought against him since the Uganda project, then the series of bitter experiences with supporters which like Pinsker he had gone through. On a still deeper stratum of the soul, however, than this suffering at the hands of others he was being eaten away by the conflict inside himself. The antithesis Jewish State –Zion is one only of the forms it takes. But it is here that Herzl's tragedy appears unveiled.

Since then the Zionist movement has only apparently liberated itself from the antithesis between a Jewish state and Zion. This antithesis must not be confused with that between the striving after other territories and the striving after Palestine. The nature of the antithesis is manifested within the Palestine movement itself and within Palestine. It was not a question of whether the house to be created here was to have the character of a state or not, it was not that that divided men's minds, it was rather a question of whether, whilst building on ' Zion ', one sees the hidden Zion that the prophets *made visible* by de- manding it,—sees it as the master-builder sees his ground-plan. ' Jewish state' versus ' Zion' means in Palestine too power without faithfulness. Power without faith is life without a meaning. Admittedly, one must not forget that faith also has a social and humanitarian form, that it embraces an obligation to righteousness internally and externally, but the looking unto the hidden Zion cannot be replaced by even the noblest social and humanitarian idea. Why can Zion be built only in Palestine? Because it is the structure hidden in the material of this land to the perfection of which this people can bring this land if it allows itself to be perfected by it: Zion means a destiny of mutual perfecting. It is not a calculation but a command; not an idea but a hidden figure waiting to be revealed. Israel would lose its own self if it replaced Palestine by another land and it would lose its own self if it replaced Zion by Palestine.

The Doctrine of the Centre
(*On Ahad-Ha'am*)

IT IS usual to regard Ahad-Ha'am as the creator of a ' cultural Zionism 'whose essential difference from ' political Zionism ' is said to consist in the fact that the latter aspires to the setting up of a Jewish state whereas cultural Zionism merely aims at a ' spiritual centre ', which, in spite of Ahad Ha'am's own inter- pretation, there is a fondness for taking as meaning a centre consisting of intellectuals. This mistake, convenient as it is, has not been removed either by what Ahad-Ha'am himself did in an attempt to refute it, or by what has been done since in this direction. Ahad-Ha'am cannot be discussed in the context of this book, however, without a clarification of the true facts of the case by way of introduction.

Ahad-Ha'am's Zionism is not 'smaller' than the political brand but greater. He demands not less, but more. He too strives for the founding of a Jewish community in Palestine, indeed he does not even object to the term ' Jewish state '; and he too envisages this foundation as taking the form of a 'great mass settlement'. But he sees this mass settlement as the organic centre of a great and living association of world Jewry, which will be able to live thanks to this organic centre. For political Zionism the future of the Diaspora is equally problematical whether a Jewish community arises in Palestine or not; it is inclined to regard it as a being condemned to fade away. For Ahad-Ha'am, on the other hand, the future of the Diaspora depends on the future of a Jewish Palestine; not, it is true, as far as its material existence is concerned, but the hope is obviously that a world Jewry concentrated in a strong, productive com- munity will be able to hold its own materially as well as spiritually. For him the Diaspora and Palestine are therefore not two different spheres, as they are for political Zionism, but a single body.

Thus the essential difference between Ahad-Ha'am and political Zionism lies not in the size of the claim they make for Palestine but in the underlying motif and the method.

Reduced to its shortest formula the difference in the under- lying motif consists in the fact that Ahad Ha'am is a true Zionist, or, as he himself would probably have put it, that he really is a true 'lover of Zion', that what he 'loves' really is Zion'. Zion has ceased long ago to be a geographical term and a poetic metaphor; in eighteen centuries of popular yearning and popular hope it has become the name for the substance of the land of Israel in the state of the yearned-for and hoped-for perfection: 'Zion' means what is intended by this land and what it is to become. Whoever loves Zion, loves a potential perfection and is bound to help make this potentiality a reality. This in itself implies that it is not a question of a spiritual essence, of a pure idea far removed from the political sphere: the 'political' is a precondition of the realization of the ideal, no less but also no more. For political Zionism the state is the goal and Zion a 'myth' which merely fires the masses; for the lover of Zion like Ahad-Ha'am the state is merely the way to the goal called Zion.

The task conceived in this way necessarily influences the method: the character of the goal must, if the 'course of things' is not to frustrate its fulfilment, influence the very first steps. It is from this angle that Ahad-Ha'am's much misunderstood doctrine of selection is to be understood. That is why he warned so emphatically against 'gathering a heap of stones in the land, without separating the whole from the broken, without order and unity and a definite pattern', and insisted that the future of the building depends on every single stone in the foundations and demanded that every effort be made to see that 'the immigrants, especially the first, should not be a hotch-potch', but 'healthy, efficient and honest men who love work and live in peace and righteousness'.

If one thinks over these two points Ahad-Ha'am's conception of the task and his conception of the method, one notices very clearly how fundamentally *realistic* his way of thinking is. The goal, as he conceives it, is not in the slightest what Zionists like to call an 'intellectual luxury'; the fact is that he is in no sense demanding a superfluity that might possibly come later on, instead of being intent on the necessities of life. Ahad-Ha'am thinks however that, if Israel were to remain content with the so-called necessities of life, it would not attain to a new life at all. He says on one occasion with great clarity that it all boils down to one single question: 'the question of existence. And to this question we answer truly—and there is no other answer: Love Zion!' In order wholly to understand this answer to the 'question of existence', one must remember the full content of Ahad-Ha'am's conception of Zion. It is impossible to achieve the 'necessities' except in connection with the 'superfluous'. If Israel reduces Zion to 'a Jewish community in Palestine,' it will not get the community. If it only wants to have a land like other lands, then the land will sink down under its feet just as the nation will melt away if it only wants to be a nation like other nations. That Ahad-Ha'am realized this is not to be ascribed to some 'idealism' or other, but to his realism: he took seriously the special conditions of the Jewish nature and Jewish history, he saw that something new to history has grown out of them, a 'new thought', a 'way that no one has ever trod before', and he saw Israel at the same time sick and wretched as it is and only to be saved by the will to perfection. Hence the need for the advance party of the elite, hence the need for the 'work of priests'. This is no 'intellectual work' but simply work, work which demands the complete surrender of self.

The transformation of the people must proceed from this work and this self-surrender of the Lovers of Zion. The *people* must learn to love Zion; so long as such love is lacking 'we lack the foundation on which alone the land can be rebuilt'. The whole heart of the people must be caught up in this burning love. It is characteristic of Ahad-Ha'am that he fears that the name 'love of Zion', as it is used in everyday speech, is too narrow, since those who use it mostly have merely a territory, namely the land of Palestine, in mind; but what is at stake is 'Judaism itself in its totality', one that now has a centre and has set out again on the road to its perfection by virtue of this centre. The love which the 'priests', the pioneers, kindle in the hearts of the people by their life, their work and their devotion is the love for the uniqueness which is represented by this people and this land, and by their association one with another.

How seriously Ahad-Ha'am was concerned with this uniqueness, how much he considered it a matter of immediate significance, is most forcibly expressed at the end of his essay on Moses where the flame of his enthusiasm which had hitherto been kept down by his zeal for truth and his realism blazes up without restraint. 'We see,' he says there, 'the "awakening" of

Moses breaking through again and ascending, and the spirit that
called Moses millennia ago and sent him on his mission against
his will—it now calls again to the late generation: "And what
rises in your mind will not happen, ye who say: 'We want to
be like the [other] nations.' As true as I live, with a strong hand
I will rule you." '

One cannot help remembering what is further announced to
the people in the chapter in Ezekiel (20) from which these words
are taken: its transfer to the 'desert of the nations', the plead-
ing with it 'face to face', the elimination of the unfaithful and
the bringing home of the faithful. One must also remember what
follows on from the above-quoted declaration of Israel's that
it wants to become like the other nations: 'in order to serve
wood and stone'. These words are certainly no longer part of
what is quoted as the utterance of Israel, but the speaker, God,
adds them, meaning by them, that is what you had in mind,
you were concerned with idols. Ahad-Ha'am left this out in his
quotation, presumably because he preferred to avoid the
religious in the narrower sense of the word, though he awaited
a religious revival too from a future Jewish life in Palestine. It
is obvious, however, that with the phrase about 'being like the
other nations' he was not simply thinking of what is usually
called 'assimilation': God pleads with Israel not because they
want to serve strange gods, but because they want to serve wood
and stone which are not gods at all,—not because they are
turning to strange, but to false, values; the important thing is
not that they should turn to their own values but to the truth:
the truth which is indeed their own truth, made known and
assigned to them. Far removed as it is from Ahad-Ha'am's
intention to make the 'love of Zion' a means of religious revival,
nevertheless the heart of his hope for the return of Israel to
Zion is obviously that out of it there may emerge a new turning
of Israel to the truth, a new revelation of the truth to Israel.
That is why he sees no less than the 'awakening of Moses'
breaking through and rising up again.

Since such great matters, the renewal of the Truth and the
renewal of Life are at stake, the land on which the hope is
fixed can be no other than the land of Israel. 'We lift our eyes
to Zion', we read in Ahad-Ha'am's reply to the project for the
foundation of a Jewish community in East Africa, 'and to
Zion alone, not from a free choice, but from a natural com-

pulsion. For we believe in perfect faith, that it is only there that
our spirit can become strong and pure and our inner powers
awake.' To create a new civilization is what Ahad-Ha'am here
calls the goal; but what he is ultimately thinking of is the
rediscovery of a living relationship to the Truth.

And yet this is the very place in which the limitations of
Ahad-Ha'am's insight become evident. The words ' only there '
which I have just quoted are followed by the declaration : ' in
the power of the historical feeling that unites the people and the
land.' That is almost the very object in question; it is not yet
really the object itself, however. Like all feelings, a *feeling* for
history can be deceptive; all kinds of things can be built on a
historical feeling, but not a certainty. The decisive question is
the objective reality which is mirrored in the historical feeling. Is
it merely a historical reality, transient like all merely historical
things, capable of being annulled by new historical facts like all
merely historical things? Or is what has befallen this people in
its encounter with this land and this land in its encounter with
this people, the token and expression of a supra-historical relationship? Is the ' election ' of this people and this land for one
another and for a third something that embraces them both and
is greater than both of them—is the Election of which the Scriptures tell, which the Haggada interprets, of which the voices
of the Exiles sing and which they discuss, an illusion, or is it a
true picture of the Eternal, drawn with the strokes of history?
It is difficult for those who live today in a time in which Eternity
is eclipsed, to cherish a belief in such a true picture. But this is
precisely what is needed. Faith alone will obtain the proof that
it is true.

THE RENEWAL OF HOLINESS
(On Rav Kook)

THE significance of the regaining of the land of Israel by the
people of Israel is to be understood on three levels, each of
which, however, only reveals its full meaning in connection
with the other two. On the first level it is acknowledged that the
people can only in the land achieve its own existence again; on
the second, that it is only there that it will rediscover its own
work, the free creative function of its spirit; on the third, that
it needs the land in order to regain its holiness. The first stage,
taken by itself, results in a narrow political view, the second by

itself in a narrow intellectual view and the third by itself in a
narrow religious view. All three must be taken together if we
are to understand what is meant by the re-birth of the Jewish
people. The first stage, including the other two, was expressed
by Hess and then in our own time in a new and extended form,
in which it is linked up with cosmic being, by A. D. Gordon;[1] the
second, taking the first into consideration and pointing forward
to the third, especially by Ahad-Ha'am; the man who did justice
in the most comprehensive and profound way to the third in
relation to the other two, is Rav Kook. He, in whose person, as
in that of no other contemporary, the holy substance of Israel
has been incorporated, acknowledged the claims of holiness in
the national movement to a greater extent than anyone else in
the Zionist thought of our time, without making it the object
of a constricting religious requirement. He related it organically
to the postulates of the independent existence of the nation and
free spiritual creativity. Furthermore, he connected it with the
postulate of the Zionist idea apparently furthest removed from
it, that of the return to nature, of a new synthesis of nature and
spirit. Fundamentally he is not concerned so much with the
continuation of an existing holiness as with a true renewal.
And for him holiness means not a sphere above life, but the
renewal of life's wholeness and unity and the transfiguration of
this wholeness and unity.

Rav Kook's particular elaboration of the Zionist idea is based
on the uniqueness and eternity of the relationship between the
people and the land in Israel, which in our age has been understood more deeply by him than by anyone else. 'This eternal
property cannot be measured with the spans of earthly time, for
it is an original and eternal property.' 'The sacred association
of Israel with its holy land is not like the natural tie which binds
all peoples and tongues to their lands.' Everywhere else the connection is the result of history: a people gains a footing in a
land and gradually, furthered by all the events of a shared
historical life, a love for this land arises which is transmitted to
the hearts of successive generations. The situation here is
different: even before Israel becomes a people, the family which
is to become a people learns, in the land in which it has not
settled but is merely a wandering guest, by a mysterious Promise

[1] On him see the next chapter, p. 154 ff.

that the land is preordained for it, and feels that a bond has
been made that can never be loosed. History can in this case
only confirm and develop what has been established in pre-
historical times, in fact in Nature itself. The eternity of Israel
is founded on the divine Nature in the character of this land.
Everything that has happened to this day and will happen for
all future time follows from that. 'The soul of the people and
the land work together to build up the elements of their common
existence, they demand that their task may be given them in
order to realize the desire for their holiness.' That is why the
love for the land is the foundation of the doctrine : ' it achieves
the consummation of the wholeness of the people of God and
the wholeness of the whole world.' And because the connection
is of such a vital and original nature, because the land is so
' attached by its innermost qualities to the reality of the people ',
neither its holiness nor the love for it can be understood by
reason alone. One must honour the mystery as a mystery in
order to approach it. Because this basic attitude and thereby
the knowledge of the mysteries has been surrendered, knowledge
of the holiness of the land of Israel has become ' blurred.'

The reality of the holy can only be grasped from the standpoint of the mystery. Then one sees that the holy is not a segre-
gated, isolated sphere of Being, but signifies the realm open to all
spheres, in which they can alone find fulfilment. The face of
the holy is not turned away from but towards the profane; it
does not want to hover over the profane but to take it up into
itself. 'The mysteries always teach us to combine the holy with
the profane.' The strict division between them has its place not
in the character and attitude of the holy but in those of the
profane; it is the profane which makes a fundamental and un-
surmountable division between itself and the holy, and on the
other side the inadequate ' usual ' holiness consists only in being
separate from the profane, whereas the perfectly holy thinks and
wills nothing but unity. The contradictions between the spheres
of the holy and the profane exist only in the subjectivity of man
who has not yet attained to spiritual unity and is unable, with
his limited powers of understanding, to mediate between the
two. In reality the main purpose of life is to raise everything
that is profane to the level of the holy. This is the stage of the
supreme Zaddikim—'true Zaddikim must be natural men ', says

Rav Kook—and it is given to the world in their highest perfection. It is this that is being prepared in the womb of the mystery.
Since this is so, ' the great national movement in Israel that is
moving in the footsteps of redemption must drink in from the
world of the hidden, from that topmost root where the holy is
firmly established with the profane in a single whole '.

The innermost essence of this great task is, however, only
revealed in the relationship to nature and the natural. There is a
kind of holiness which declares war, as on the profane in general,
so in particular on Nature and everything natural as something
that must be suppressed in order to attain to holiness. But the
world, and above all scattered and broken Israel is in need of
Nature. Israel needs the natural life that it has lost; it needs it in
order to attain to the true and perfect holiness. For the segre-
gated holiness that has always acted contrary to Nature, and
has oppressed and perverted it and is now hurriedly assembling
the remains of its power to fight Nature, is not the perfect
holiness; it has resulted from a splitting up of Nature and spirit
which is foreign to the purpose of Creation, it is the hallowing
of the separated spirit alone. In reality it does not fight the
great world of Nature at all, it does not see and does not know
it; what it struggles against is its own nature, that is, the residue
of Nature that still adheres to it and from which it wants to rid
itself. It cannot win this battle; the imperfect holiness ' stumbles
and falls in its struggle '. The separate and independent holiness of the spirit, as opposed to the holiness of Nature, arose in
Israel when the people was removed from its soil and reduced
to the preservation of spirituality as such; it was then that those
concerned with eternal life separated themselves from the life
of the passing hour. This ability to set holiness against Nature
was made possible because the Shekhina came down with Israel
into the exile. But as against all separation of Nature from the
spirit, so too against this separation of the spirit from Nature
there is a protest from Heaven. The original source of the holy
itself, the Light of the world requires of the world in general
and of scattered and broken Israel in particular the ennoblement
of nature, of the simple life, of its health, and of normality in
all the functions of life. The mystery of the national movement
of Israel, the mystery of the return of the people to its land, is
grounded in this requirement.

It must be admitted that the naturalness that is awakened
by the demand of holiness that comes from above but of which
it is conscious only as an inner voice, and by which it feels
called upon to ennoble itself, falters. It has an innermost desire
for the supreme holiness, the 'holiness of silence', of pure
existence, but instead of rising to the holy and so finding and
realizing its own holiness, it feels the holy as its opponent and
obstruction, it hates it and rebels against it. But this holy against
which it rises so wrathfully is not the perfect holiness but the
separated, 'everyday' holiness: Nature hates the holy by which
it is oppressed and perverted. In reality the separated spirituality
and separated naturalness fight against each other; they fight
each other instead of each giving the other what it needs and so
helping to establish the kingdom of perfect holiness. And like the
separated holy in its struggle against Nature, separated naturalness must also stumble and fall in its fight against holiness.

Even though the rebellion of Nature is, to begin with,
abortive, nevertheless its great importance must be fully recognized. No one in the camp of the Zionist idea has expressed the
significance of the regeneration of the body with such spiritual
power and from such a spiritual depth as Rav Kook. 'We have
forgotten the holiness of the body,' he says, 'we have forgotten
that we have a holy flesh, that we have it no less than we have
a holy spirit. We have forsaken the active life and the purification of the senses and the association with bodily, sensual reality,
because of a degenerate fear, because of a lack of faith in the
holiness of the land.' The conversion of Israel can succeed only
if, in union with all the glory of the spiritual it is 'also a bodily
conversion, creating healthy blood, healthy flesh, well-chiselled,
well-founded bodies, a flaming mind radiant over strong muscles
and shining in the power of the hallowed flesh, which had been
weakened, the soul, pointing to the bodily resurrection of the
dead'. As such great things are at stake, even the abortive
exaltation of the natural must be accepted, since it makes a
beginning. The fact that it is taking place in the land of Israel
or at any rate with the land in mind is a guarantee that it
will be led into the right way; it is here, in fact, that the holiness
of nature remained hidden when Israel took the holiness of the
spirit, and it alone, into exile. 'It has come down to us', Rav
Kook says, 'that there will be a spiritual rebellion in the land of

Israel and in Israel in the period in which the beginning of national re-birth takes place.' A 'fleshy-minded thoughtlessness' which injures the life of the soul and 'diminishes' it will then come over the section of the people which desires nothing but the restoration of the national existence and is quite content if it lives to see the way being prepared for that. The spirit rebels against its own holiness. But, bitter and serious as this state of affairs is for everyone familiar with the nature of perfect holiness, all must realize that the rebellion proceeded from a tremendous need. The turning towards the material had to arise in the people in such a violent form because of the long periods of time in which it was bereft of the natural association with material things. Certainly, 'when this inclination is born, it will stride about enraged and stir up storms', but these will be the birth-pangs of the Messiah. 'The audacity in the time before the coming of the Messiah is a diminution of the light, but one which serves the redemption of the world.' 'The sons of the audacious', Rav Kook says, 'who break through the barriers, will stand in the high radiance of the first man, they will be prophets of the supreme degree to whom and through whom the tree of life is wholly revealed.'

At this point the teaching of Rav Kook attains both a peculiar boldness and a peculiar depth. What the youth of Israel, he declares, do to strengthen their bodies in the land of Israel in order to become sturdy sons of the people promotes, all un-known to them, the spiritual power of the supreme Zaddikim whose concern is with the uniting of the holy names, that is, with the combining of the various powers of holiness; for, through the perfecting of the body a purer form of Nature is provided for the work of these men. When the boys play here, they not only contribute to the strength of the people: this playing is 'a holy service which raises the Shekhina higher and higher, just as it is raised by hymns and praises'. In the latter case the inward substance is developed, in the former case the outward, 'and both together perfect all the orders of holiness', as is written (Proverbs 3, 6): 'Thou shalt know Him in all His ways.' No doubt there are grave weaknesses in the lives of those who have devoted themselves to the bodily strengthening of the people; no doubt their thought and action lack insight into the nature of the holy and its original source. But it must not be

overlooked that today ' in the footsteps of the Messiah ', when his
coming is being visibly prepared, ' the Nefesh, the vital soul of
those who have deserted the faith of Israel, but who have, in love,
joined the cause of the people, the land and the re-birth of
Israel, has reached a higher degree of perfection than the Nefesh
of the faithful who do not possess this advantage of an essential feeling for the whole, for the reconstruction of the people
and the land ',—though it must be admitted that the Ruach, the
spiritual soul, stands far higher in the latter than in the former.
Both souls are indispensable for the Messianic work of perfection, both are useless in isolation, they are dependent on each
other, they must come to one another in order to become useful.
Only then can Israel become ' One Union ' and in the consum-
mating influence of the Nefesh of the good deserters from the
faith on the Nefesh of the faithful and of the Ruach of the pious
on the Ruach of the disloyal in the light of the Messiah, the
Neshama, the united soul whose bearers are the supreme
Zaddikim, will attain its perfect development. ' I see with my
own eyes ', Rav Kook writes, ' the light of the life of Elijah
rising, more and more revealing its power towards its God, the
holiness in Nature breaks through its barriers, it goes out in
power to join the Holy that is above Nature . . . Elijah has come
to proclaim peace . . . We are all coming near to Nature and
Nature is coming near to us.'

The power, however, that is alone able to prepare the Nefesh
and the Ruach, the separated principle of Nature and the
separated principle of the holy for each other, is the power of
the land of Israel. For this land has the power that transforms.
It rightly bears the name of Canaan, the name of the ' corrupted
and accursed man '. Chosen for great and holy things, it has
transformed the gross inheritance of Canaan into great and holy
things. The high treasure of life that is hidden in the recesses
of darkness has been unearthed by the inner power of this land,
stamped by the eternal divine vow of Election. It will also prove
its force of reviving and transforming in Israel itself, will prepare
its two separated powers for one another and bring them to
one another. It was in this land that the Holy once implanted
itself in Nature; ever since, the air of this land, has, according
to the words of the sages, the power to make men wise, that is
to say: it illuminates the soul, and enables it ' to understand

the principle of the *united world*'. It is here that the Israelite view of the world and life once grew, which is fundamentally ' the growing mastery of the united over the divided world '. It is this mastery of the united and the divided world that will now take place as a result of the reborn power of the land first of all in Israel itself and then throughout the whole human race.

Only then will, so Rav Kook prophesies, Nature reveal itself again to the Israelite poet in all its glory. ' From the day ', the wise men say, ' on which the sanctuary was destroyed, the firmament has not been visible in its purity.' The time will come when it will be visible again.

A Man who realizes the Idea of Zion
(*On A. D. Gordon*)

OF ALL those who came to the land in the period of new settlement the man Ahron David Gordon appears to me to be the most remarkable. Compared with the others he seems like a natural phenomenon, where they seem like merely social phenomena. Even those who rebel against society are bound to it by the very fact of rebelling against it; but a man like Gordon is exceptional in that he seems to associate directly with the powers of Nature and not merely indirectly by way of social forms. This is an occurrence of extraordinary rarity in the Jewish people. Just as Gordon is independent *vis-à-vis* society, he is independent *vis-à-vis* history. Unlike some of his contemporaries and comrades he no more rebels against history than he does against society; he has assimilated history, he lives on it but it has no programmatic value for him, positive or negative. To be sure, he bears the same burden as all other Jews; he has brought it with him into the land; but it neither weighs him down, nor does he throw his head up in the air to show that he has rid himself of it: the man who throws his head up in the air is not free, whereas Gordon bears the burden and is yet free at the same time. There are some who approach him in this but none that equals him; he is without peer in the Jewry of our day.

The spiritual motives that have brought other settlers to Palestine (I am disregarding the traditional religious motives for the present), such as the demand for national freedom and independence, for the establishment on the land of a wander-

ing people, for the overcoming of parasitism, for an autonomous way of life, are naturally not unknown to Gordon's heart.
But behind all these social and historical principles and over-
shadowing them all, there stands a basically human principle,
or rather not a principle at all but a basically human longing:
the demand for a life truly in accordance with Nature. It is quite
true that this is also historically conditioned: the Jews have lost
the life lived in true accordance with Nature and they want to
get it back again; but something has nevertheless come to life
here that is still deeper than all the historical strata of existence,
deeply though they penetrate, something from the depths of
man as man. This demand is not merely that of a Jew, it is that
of a man. And, for all that, it is quite unsentimental and un-
romantic. It does not mourn for a paradise stolen from us by
civilization, it proclaims man's everlasting claim not to be cut off
from mother Nature by human nature, however it develops. The
aim of this demand is no mere enjoyment of Nature, no merely
contemplative feelings, this man has no desire to lose himself
to the Cosmos in blissful self-forgetfulness but he does want to
participate in its life, in the life of the cosmos itself. The real
wound in Gordon's heart is caused by the Jews having fallen not
from political self-determination but from the Cosmos. No
merely receptive behaviour will enable them to find their place
in it again. Man can participate in the Cosmos only when he
does something in the cosmic context that is his particular sphere,
just as the stars revolve in their courses and the trees grow
towards the sun. To work on the land entrusted to his care is
what befits man. The men sent by a newly arising Israel to
work on the soil of its land represent its reunion, not merely
with the earth but with the Cosmos.

When he came to the land Gordon himself did not move
from an existence without Nature to one with Nature. He had
lived in a Podolian village before he became part of the life of
a Palestinian village. But his life in the Podolian village did not
satisfy him, for it was the life of an 'overseer'. To inspect the
work of others working on the land is not the same as truly
participating in cosmic life. The man whose task is to see that
other men work well has not yet achieved the right and perfect
relationship to Nature. Gordon, the official in the Podolian
village, still feels like a parasite towards Nature. For him the way

to Palestine is the way out of a mere contemplation of Nature to organic participation in her life. It is the way leading to work with his own hands. Gordon goes to Palestine as a man who no longer wants to enjoy Nature with his eyes alone or merely to supervise the work of other hands. Eyes and hands belong together. Only the man who lives in Nature with his whole being truly lives in her. Man becomes whole by working in Nature with his own body. Israel will restore the wholeness of human nature through the work of its people in the natural world of the countryside.

Gordon cannot be understood as coming from the Slav world. The Slav has not yet sensed the kind of problems that determined the path taken by Gordon. Even Tolstoy, who of all Slav intellectuals was probably the one to feel most strongly the relationship between man and the earth, did not penetrate to this quite simple and at the same time exceedingly deep problem of man's gaining his place in the Cosmos through active participation in its life. It seems to me as though a few important Americans, such as Henry Thoreau, the proclaimer of the ' duty of civil disobedience ', and Walt Whitman, the poet of democratic comradeship, came nearer to Gordon,—a possibility that the problems of American civilization make it not difficult to account for. When I read in Thoreau that the chief thing is ' to see man as an inhabitant, or a parcel of Nature, rather than a member of society ' I seem to hear the voice of Gordon. But for these Americans Nature is nevertheless still fundamentally the landscape, it is not so really and truly the Cosmos as for Gordon. In their words I see the trees more clearly than the stars. In Gordon's I see the stars, even when he is only speaking of the trees. Talk about a ' cosmic consciousness ' is no rare thing in American literature, but it sounds to me like an abstraction which is more likely to lead one away from Gordon's simple and practical formulation of the question. And when I think of Whitman or Thoreau, I see them wandering, gloriously wandering, but I do not see them hoeing and weeding like Gordon. In saying this I am not forgetting of course that Thoreau takes a hand on his farm for all he is worth. But when he does so he does not yet really know what he is doing. Gordon, on the other hand, does know what he is doing. He knows that his work enables man to participate in the life of the Cosmos.

This is something entirely different from a 'cosmic consciousness'. Gordon's knowledge is a faith and his faith is a life.
Therefore his word is only one of the functions of his life, the
one by which his life is expressed, by which this kind of life is
expressed. His words will be preserved from one generation to
another in indissoluble association with his memory. Thus it was
too with Whitman. But the unique significance of this unity of
word and life in Gordon is based on the fact that he was what
Whitman was not and could not be by reason of the whole
historical situation in which he lived: the pioneer of his people
on the way to a renewed participation in the life of the Cosmos.
Whitman sings the praises of pioneering, he cries: 'Fresh and
strong the world we seize, world of labour and the march,
pioneers! O Pioneers!'; but Gordon *is* the pioneer, and he says
only what he is. Whitman too never tires of praising work, and
he rightly says in his 'concluding words', the 'backward glance
o'er travel'd roads': 'the working-man and working-woman
were to be in my pages from first to last'; but only Gordon
can say: 'Our way—to Nature through work!', and he is
only stating the way he treads himself,—as a pioneer. Whitman
declares: 'The ambitious thought of my song is to help the
forming of a great aggregate Nation'; Gordon, who was no
poet but a genuine speaker, that is to say, the mouthpiece of
a reality in process of becoming, does not attribute such great
influence to words, yet of the spirit that inspires his actions and
therefore his words, of the spirit of a 'new, essential, cosmic
relationship to Nature and to life', he says, not at all ambitiously,
in the genuinely Gordonian manner, with a quite unemotional
'perhaps' in the midst of the expression of emotion: 'Perhaps
this is the spirit that will bring new life to the dry bones and
to the rotting bones too.' The way to Nature is the way to the
resurrection of the people.

    With these presuppositions of Gordon's in mind it is under-
standable that he was better able than anyone else in the modern
Jewish national movement to renew the insight into the unique
relationship between the people and the land of Israel. 'To open
the new account with Nature', without which 'we who have
been torn away from Nature, we who have already forgotten
the taste of natural life' cannot achieve a new life, will succeed
only in Israel's own land. 'A lively and labouring people needs

to imbibe from its roots—and the roots are in the land of Israel.'
It is more than a merely historical inheritance that has now to be
taken possession of, more than a continuity interrupted by an
historical age that has to be restored: with intuitive force
Gordon recognizes that the mystery of Israel's existence is bound
up with the mystery of this land. He beholds this mystery as
he beholds the land. ' It seems ', Gordon notes in Judea, ' as if
the whole nature of the plenitude from on high that is poured
from all worlds into the soul of man, but especially into the soul
of the Jew, is entirely different from what it is in the lands of
the Diaspora. In the language of the soul—but only in the
language of the soul—I would say that the nature of Truth, of
Holiness, of Beauty, of Power, the nature of all spheres is
open to the soul in another way, in another state, and that they
combine with one another in different combinations.' And
further: ' It seems to you that the frontiers between the manifest
and the hidden are very much wider and deeper here in the
world of the nation that is the daughter of this Nature, than in
other worlds: the place where the hidden begins in the world
of the others is here in the quality of that Biblical ' purity as of
the core of heaven '. I can remember no passage in modern
literature where such a significant feeling of the elemental
share of the land in the faith, doctrine and message of Israel
is expressed. Gordon emphasizes: ' Only in the language of the
soul.' He means that he does not venture into the sphere of
Transcendence, that he wants to make a statement not about
Being itself but merely about the experience of Being. Gordon is
one of those who do not consider it proper in this age of the
' eclipse of the luminaries ' to utter names; no attitude is more
remote than this from the dominant atheistic convention of our
day. Gordon knows the meaning and influence of the lack of
faith in our world. ' We lack the religious relation in our national
work, the relation that produces mighty religions which renew
the face of the world, and hence we lack religious faith in everything we do.' These words must not be taken pragmatically.
Gordon is not concerned that the people should regain ' religion '
because religion has such a favourable and constructive influence
on the life and work of the people. All ' as ifs ' are alien to his
soul. The ' main thing ', Gordon says, is to establish for ourselves a new relationship ' to the mystery of existence and life '.

The mystery of existence—by which Gordon means not a pro-
visional mystery to be unravelled as we progress in knowledge,
but one that, in accordance with its own nature and our nature,
will not cease to remain a mystery to us—is no fiction, no
intellectual formation, but an original and prime reality and it
is a basic condition of the people's re-birth that it should attain
an authentic and steadfast relationship to it. And this again is
closely connected with the land. Just as Israel can only participate
in the life of the Cosmos there, so too it is only there that it can
regain a religious relationship to the mystery of existence.
'David's harp can only regain its power here in the land of
Israel.' By that Gordon meant more than lyric poetry or even
art or the 'creative faculty' in general. What we have in mind
when we say 'David', is not 'a religious poet', but a man who
has intercourse with Eternity and who sings so that the *voice*
of the soul may not be lacking in this intercourse in which the
soul gives everything it has.

Gordon did not acquire his deep insight into the relationship
between the people and the land all at once. Probably no one
else has ever suffered and struggled so much to attain it, which in
the case of such a man, whose very life was his real way to
knowledge, means that probably no one has ever suffered and
struggled so much for the sake of his own relationship to the
land. His own utterances allow us to glimpse four stages of this
life-process and it is only as we look at this development that
we see his teaching in its true light.

When he comes to the land—as we have said, not from a
life without Nature into a life with Nature, but from one
Nature into another—he finds it difficult to grasp the new things,
the things of his own that had been lost once. He had become
quite intimate with the Russian countryside, he had understood
it, just as he felt that it understood him, he had felt that it was
like a 'simple, naïve and loving mother'. Not so the Palestinian
countryside. It too is a mother and its love is probably still
deeper but it is infinitely aloof, it is as a king's daughter who
looks with silent grief at the child that has grown up, tormented
and depraved by slavery in foreign lands, and has now returned
to her; 'she understands you well in her wise heart, but you are
not competent to understand her'. And Gordon remarks: the
Jews who live here do not yet understand the land they are

living in, they are remote from it, they are still distinct from it. Gordon realizes the depth of the gulf that has opened up between the people and the land : even when they are together again, it still continues.

After the first five years his views have changed. He still feels again and again : 'The land of my fathers is far and strange to me and I am far and strange to it.' But one thing makes him now directly aware of the relation of mother and son : he has seen the devastation of the land with his own eyes, and it is that same devastation that he finds in his soul. 'The devastation,' he cries to himself, *is* the devastation of your soul and the corrupter is the corrupter who has ruled in your life . . . you stand before your own fate.' In the ruins of the mother's face Gordon finds his own ruined face again. Distance is overcome by contemplation of the selfsame lot. The land has not waited in sublime majesty for its far-off sons, it has been dishonoured like them, they find each other again in the one grief that has taken different forms, and in the one common hope.

And again about five years later Gordon gives expression to the decisive step he has taken meanwhile and which was the legitimate continuation of the two former steps, the continuation on the true way. Once again the image of mother and child recurs, but in the place of ' distance ' between the two there is a new nearness, and reciprocity has taken the place of mere equality. 'The mother Erets Israel', Gordon writes at the beginning of the first Great War in the first of his 'Letters from Palestine ', ' claims your body and life or she claims nothing. It is not my purpose to direct your attention to what you should and could do for Palestine, but to what Palestine can do for you. . . . Only when you begin to look for something, that something that no Jew can find anywhere else. . . . only then will you be competent to do something, something of vital importance for Palestine.' Here the uniqueness of the mutual relationship between this people and this land is recognized and expressed in the form which it has assumed in this hour of destiny, in the present actuality of the relationship. More than ever before the land claims everything of the people, in order to give it everything. Once again the reciprocity comes into light in the form of a decision, a decision—nobody knew this better than Gordon —to begin not merely an ' independent ' but a true life, a life in the truth of Nature and work, of righteousness and faith.

And again five more years pass, and Gordon speaks—at a conference in Prague, at which I saw him for the first and last time—a word that shows how still nearer the land and he have come to one another. 'It is not we,' he says, 'it is our land, that speaks to the people. We have merely to express and intimate the words spoken by the land, and we say to you, to the whole people: the land is waiting for you.' Instead of mere reciprocity we are here confronted with an absolute identification. Gordon has become the mouth of the land. How many orators may have adopted such an attitude in this age! But Gordon is no master of oratory but a master of life, and what he utters is no mere attitude, but the very reality of his life. He has really merged into one with the land, it has indeed empowered him to speak for it, just as a man's heart empowers his mouth, so he has become the mouth of the land. After having first merely admired the land from a distance, he had come to see the common fate shared by both the land and himself, then he had come to see their relationship as one of mutual exchange and now as one of physical connection in the way that the heart and mouth are connected. This was the final stage in the sixteen-year-long process of suffering and struggle. Two years later he died. 'We have only *one* comfort', Gordon says in that letter, after he has described the 'pettiness' of the Jews of Palestine faced with the greatness of the task, '. . . that we feel our pains thoroughly. We are like a woman, who for a long time had no children, however much she besought God—and who suddenly notices that she is pregnant. She rejoices over every pain and only fears that the pain may be too light, since perhaps it is not the real pain. In the Diaspora we did not feel *these* pains.' With this very metaphor, a Hasidic leader, Rabbi Israel of Rizin had once spoken of the redemption. But Gordon is right: these pains were not felt in the Diaspora. Gordon's own existence attests that they are the pains of childbirth.

BIOGRAPHICAL APPENDIX

BIOGRAPHICAL APPENDIX

AHAD-HA'AM (i.e. 'One of the People,' pseudonym of Asher Ginzberg) : the leading thinker in the modern Hebrew national movement, 1856–1927.

BAAL-SHEM-TOV, i.e. the 'Master of the Good Name,' the description of the founder of the great religious movement of Eastern Jewry known as Hasidism, Rabbi Israel ben Elieser, 1770–1760. Cf. my book *Tales of the Hasidism*, 1 (1946), pp. 11 ff, 35 ff.

EDMUND : see Rothschild.

JAKOB FRANK, 1726–1791, the last and most questionable in the series of Jewish pseudo-Messiahs, worked in Podolia where he went over to Christianity. Later he lived in Offenbach. Cf. my book *Hasidism* (1948), pp. 10 ff.

A. D. GORDON, 1856–1922, went to Palestine as a farm-worker at the age of 50; the central spiritual figure in the reconstruction work of the working-class.

THEODORE HERZL, 1860–1904, the originator of political Zionism and the founder of the Zionist organization. His treatise *The Jewish State* appeared in 1896. The first Zionist Congress, of which he was the Chairman, took place in Bâle in 1897. The settlement in British East Africa (Uganda) offered to him by the British Government in 1903 was turned down by the Zionist movement after Herzl's death, but a part of the movement turned its attention to the so-called 'territorialism' which, under Zangwill's leadership, strove for a Jewish colonial enterprise with a political character outside Palestine.

MOSES HESS, 1812–1875, noted Socialist author of the generation of Marx and Engels and the first important representative of the modern elaboration of the Zionist idea. His book *Rome and Jerusalem* appeared in 1862.

BARON MORITZ HIRSCH, 1831–1896, a well-known philanthropist who especially promoted the settlement of Jews in the Argentine.

JEHUDA HALEVI, born *c.* 1083, died *c.* 1145, the great Hebrew poet of the Spanish diaspora. His work *Kusari* ('The Khazar'), written in Arabic, deals with the purpose and destiny of Jewry.

RABBI ABRAHAM JIZHAK KOOK, 1866–1935, the representative figure among the Jewish orthodoxy in Palestine.

RABBI LIVA BEN BEZALEL, born *c.* 1520, died 1609 in Prague ('The High Rabbi Loev'), one of the great Jewish philosophers of religion. Legend has glorified him as the creator of the 'Golem'.

RABBI NAHMAN OF BRAZLAV, 1771–1810, the grandson of Baal-Shem-Tov (see above), and one of the last great personalities of Hasidism. Cf. my book *The Stories of the Rabbi Nahman* (in German).

MAX NORDAU, 1849–1923, well-known writer and publicist, with Herzl the most important leader of political Zionism.

LEO PINSKER, 1831–1891, a doctor in Odessa, leader of the pre-Herzl movement of the Lovers of Zion. His treatise *Auto-emancipation* appeared in 1882.

BARON EDMUND ROTHSCHILD, 1845–1934, promoted the work of settlement in Palestine in the most generous fashion.

SABBATAI ZEWI, 1626–1676, the central figure in the strongest Messianic movement of the Diaspora which was also most important for its influence on the development of heretical ideas. Cf. especially G. Scholem, *Major Trends in Jewish Mysticism* (2nd edition, 1946), pp. 287 ff.

PEREZ SMOLENSKI, 1842–1885, famous Hebrew novelist and pioneer of the nationalist movement.

SOME TECHNICAL TERMS EXPLAINED

GALUT : Exile. Specific description of the fate of Jewry in the Diaspora.

MIDRASH : Interpretation. A form of literature based essentially on the free interpretation of the scriptures.

SHEKHINA : Indwelling. The presence of God which has descended into the world and shares its lot.

THE WISE MEN : The masters of Talmudic literature.

CORRIGENDA

BAAL-SHEM-TOV: born 1700, not 1770

BARON MORITZ HIRSCH: *for* MORITZ *read* MAURICE DE

RABBI NAHMAN OF BRAZLAV: *for* grandson *read* great-grandson

    Scholem, *Major Trends: for* 2nd edition, 1946, pp. 287 ff. *read* 3rd edition, 1954, pp. 287–324

Also, p. 113, *for* Jeuerbach *read* Feuerbach